> *"Twenty-volume folios*
> *will never make a revolution.*
> *It's the little pocket pamphlets*
> *that are to be feared."*
> **Voltaire**

FIELD (#3) NOTES

ANDREW POTTER

On Decline

Stagnation, Nostalgia, and Why

Every Year is the Worst One Ever

BIBLIOASIS
Windsor, Ontario

FIRST EDITION

Library and Archives Canada Cataloguing in Publication

Title: On decline / Andrew Potter.
Names: Potter, Andrew, author.
Description: Series statement: Field notes ; #3 | Includes bibliographical
references.
Identifiers: Canadiana (print) 20210207930 | Canadiana (ebook)
20210208260 | ISBN 9781771963947
    (softcover) | ISBN 9781771963954 (ebook)
Subjects: LCSH: Civilization, Western—21st century. | LCSH: Regression
(Civilization) | LCSH:
    History, Modern—21st century.
Classification: LCC CB245 .P68 2021 | DDC 909/.09821083—dc23

Edited by Daniel Wells
Copyedited by Emily Donaldson
Typeset by Vanessa Stauffer
Series designed by Ingrid Paulson

Published with the generous assistance of the Canada Council for the Arts,
which last year invested $153 million to bring the arts to Canadians throughout
the country, and the financial support of the Government of Canada. Biblioasis
also acknowledges the support of the Ontario Arts Council (OAC), an agency of
the Government of Ontario, which last year funded 1,709 individual artists
and 1,078 organizations in 204 communities across Ontario, for a total of
$52.1 million, and the contribution of the Government of Ontario through the
Ontario Book Publishing Tax Credit and Ontario Creates.

PRINTED AND BOUND IN CANADA

For Liz, who gives me hope

I'm not saying that David Bowie was holding the fabric of the universe together, but ... [gestures broadly at everything]

—Katie Loewy via Twitter
(@sweetestcyanide)

"You're too young to remember it," her mother said, "but we were expecting nuclear war all the time, really, up into my early thirties. Later, all of that felt unreal. But the feeling that things became basically okay turns out to have actually been what was unreal."

—William Gibson, *Agency*

Contents

Introduction: Welcome to the Jackpot

ON JANUARY 8, 2016, David Bowie gave himself a birthday gift in the form of *Blackstar*, a quirky new album that nodded toward his Krautrock period in the mid-seventies. The title track was a mix of Gregorian chants, soulful jazz, and electronica, and clocked in at a solid ten minutes. It was also a decidedly moody album, full of cryptic songs about mysticism and mortality. Critics loved it. It turned out that Bowie's birthday present was also his parting gift to the world. Two days later, he died of liver cancer. The year was off to a lousy start, and it was about to get a whole lot worse.

As a bitterly clever viral tweet suggested, it almost seemed like David Bowie had been an alien force holding the fabric of the universe together. With his death, things started to unravel on virtually every level. In Syria, the tide turned in the six-year-long civil war as Russian-backed government forces, making free use of horrific barrel bombs, captured the rebel stronghold of Aleppo. Thanks to global warming, 2016 was the hottest year on record. Hurricanes ravaged the Gulf, while the Zika virus emerged as a global threat, especially to pregnant women. There were terrorist attacks in Brussels, Nice, and at a nightclub in Orlando. In June, Britain shocked the world by voting to leave the EU, something that would have stood as the most notable political story of the year if it hadn't been eclipsed in November by the election of Donald Trump as the president of the United States.

Amidst it all there was a distressing number of high-profile celebrity deaths, as Bowie was followed into the unknown by Alan Rickman, Muhammad Ali, Carrie Fisher, Leonard Cohen, and, on Christmas Day, George Michael. Most shocking was the death, in late April, of Prince, probably the only person capable of challenging Bowie for the title of most important musician of the last half-century.

And so the pattern seemed to be set: A stable international order collapsing amid renewed Great Power machinations, populist retrenchment and decay amongst the established democracies fuelled by fake news and Russian manipulation, terror attacks abroad and mass shootings at home, and the constant menace of looming environmental catastrophe. Behind it all, marking time like a drummer in a death march, was the steady beat of dead celebrities reminding us that the old, familiar world was being replaced by something new and uncertain.

Newspapers' December wrap-ups widely agreed that 2016 was "the worst year ever."[1] And yet every year since has also felt like the worst year ever, to the point where claiming the current year as worse than the previous one has become something of a social-media cliché.

It's hard to know how much of this is just a consequence of omnipresent social media triggering the
well-known "availability heuristic," the cognitive shortcut
that causes us to rely on the examples that come most
quickly to mind when we make judgments or evaluations.
Social media is full of doom and gloom (there's a reason
why "doomscrolling"[2] was the hit neologism of 2020), so
of course we think the world is getting worse all the time.
Want to feel better about things? Try turning off your
phone for a bit, get some fresh air and exercise, play with
your kids.

Also, even if things are going really badly at the
moment, it doesn't necessarily reflect on the bigger pic-
ture. Step back for a longer view and you'll notice that the
world breaks—like, really fractures—every ten years or
so, almost without exception, and has done so for a while
now. In Europe and North America, the years 1914–1918,
1929–1933, and 1939–1945 were all followed by a two-de-
cade period of growth and relative stability. But then if we
look look at the years 1968, 1979, 1989, 2001, 2008–
2009, a decade-long cycle of disruption and instability
starts to look like the norm, not the exception. What are
we to make of this pattern? The pessimist would say:
Look at how fragile our systems are. To which the opti-
mist responds, No, look at how robust and resilient they
are. Things break but then they recover, so while it's probably never a bad idea to turn off your phone, there's really
not much to worry about.

Whatever else you might want to say about how 2020
played out, one thing you cannot seriously claim to be is
surprised. An elementary exercise in inductive reasoning
("each year is worse than the last"), combined with judi-

cious appreciation of the ten-year rule, would lead one straight to the conclusion that, no matter how bad things were by the end of 2019, they were almost certainly going to get worse.

And so they did, and they didn't waste any time getting there. On January 3, an American drone strike near Baghdad killed Qasem Suleimani, the head of the Quds Force, Iran's special operations and intelligence unit. Five days later, with tensions running very high, an Iranian missile defense battery shot down a Ukrainian Airlines flight out of Tehran, killing 176 civilians, more than half of whom were Canadians or had ties to Canada. For a while, war looked like a serious possibility.

Meanwhile, Australia continued to burn as the worst wildfires in memory consumed huge swaths of the country. There was a locust invasion in Eastern Africa, a volcano erupted in the Philippines, basketball star Kobe Bryant was killed in a helicopter crash, and US President Donald Trump's impeachment inquiry lurched towards its predetermined end. In Canada, the hereditary chiefs of the Wet'suwet'en Nation in British Columbia came out against a planned gas pipeline that would cut across part of their traditional lands. In response, mass protests and blockades organized under the hashtag #shutdowncanada closed city cores, highways, and rail lines across the country.

All of this, keep in mind, happened *before the end of February*. Vague rumblings of a scary new contagion coming out of China were at that point happening only in the background.

At first it seemed like it was going to be just one of those things. A few lines on a chyron that scrolls by and then vanishes after a few turns of the news cycle. But when pictures emerged of two new hospitals being frantically built from scratch at the epicentre of the outbreak in Wuhan, people started to pay attention. The Chinese government put the entire Hubei province, almost 60 million people, on lockdown. But by then the contagion, which experts were calling a "novel coronavirus," had spread to other countries. Northern Italy was soon under lockdown as well, and any hope that this might just fade out the way SARS or MERS had done died at the beginning of March with the release of satellite photos from Iran showing mass graves being dug in Qom to handle the coronavirus dead. With South Korea and Japan also experiencing surging cases of the virus, on March 11, 2020, the World Health Organization declared a global pandemic.

Again, no one can honestly claim to be surprised. At least not about the specifics of the pandemic (though lots of serious people, including Bill Gates, had been warning about such a thing for years), but more generally, can anyone really claim to be caught off guard by the dystopian condition into which we have stumbled?

It's time we accepted that we're in a state of decline.

* * *

AT THE BEGINNING of every apocalyptic thriller there's typically a scene where the hero is getting ready for work, feeding the kids breakfast, dealing with a dog that has barfed in the living room, and with myriad other minor stresses of everyday life. Meanwhile, on the TV or radio in the background, the news is cycling through the usual mundanities of petty crime and traffic and local weather, but thrown into the mix are a handful of Easter eggs:

warnings of nuclear sabre-rattling by jumped-up third-world dictators; quirky reports about bizarre weather patterns in Europe; alcoholic monkeys attacking tourists in India; a fun little hit about a couple from the Midwest who swore they saw an alien spacecraft collecting samples in a field behind their house.

These scenes play an important narrative function in establishing the family or relationship ties that provide an emotional connection with the audience. But they also foreshadow the plot-driving crisis to come while making it clear that the warning signs are being lost or ignored, drowned out by the noise of the 24/7 news cycle and the question of whether the pool cleaner is coming today or tomorrow, and if Madison or Skyler has soccer or piano after school.

That's why these movies always feature a lone scientist or researcher who really knows what's going on, but who is dismissed by everyone as crazy or conspiracy-minded. Their job is to both flatter the viewer (we know what's coming too!) and to warn us: there are patterns out there—in human affairs, in nature, in the cosmos—that most of us are too busy to notice. And our ignorance and indifference are leading us to our doom.

The difficulty lies in the question of how we tell the false prophets from the genuine seers. Bill Gates honourably refrained from running around yelling "I frickin' told you so," but as late as January 23, 2020, Canada's chief public health officer Theresa Tam went on the record to reassure Canadians that "the risk of an outbreak remains low," even though the military had briefed the defense minister a week earlier on the coronavirus threat. The Canadian federal cabinet didn't even meet to discuss

COVID-19 until January 27, by which time the virus had already spread beyond China's borders.

Eventually there will have to be a public reckoning in Canada and many other Western countries about their lethargic and ineffectual official response to the virus in the early weeks and months of its spread. One part of the answer will almost certainly be the difficulty of discerning the signal from the noise. The problem is notoriously acute in intelligence gathering, whether it has to do with looking for evidence of a terrorist attack or sifting data looking for signs of a public health contagion. It's worth remembering that after 9/11 there were plenty of armchair intelligence analysts pointing out that there had been clear signs of an imminent terrorist attack on American soil. It's easy to look back and cherry-pick the evidence to show the signals that were missed, but that involves deliberately ignoring the thousands of other bits of information that only in retrospect turned out to be noise.

Then there's Donald Trump. From the moment he stunned the world by winning the 2016 US presidential election, Trump dominated the news with a grenade-tossing governing style, using Twitter as his launcher of choice. The pattern typically started with Trump chumming the waters with some insane offhand tweet, often in the middle of the night while he was watching Fox news. This was inevitably followed by a social media feeding frenzy that quickly overwhelmed the news cycle.

As the rueful "but her emails" meme had it, it would have been very different if Hillary Clinton had won. Things certainly would have been a lot less crazy, even if many of Trump's opponents obviously found raw satisfaction in flipping out every time the president went golfing or praised a group of racists or insulted a military widow or forgot that Puerto Ricans are Americans. There was a smug pleasure to be had in keeping a running tally of the number of lies he told while in office, how many days he spent golfing or in Mar-a-Lago, or how many members of his administration contracted COVID-19. Donald Trump's presidency was undeniably a catastrophe for the United States and the world.

Yet the question needs to be asked whether the relentless, real-time obsessing over all things Trump distracted us from noticing the broader trends underway in our civilization; trends for which Trump was, at best, merely a symptom.

After all, every year since 2016 has followed the same general pattern: large geopolitical stressors combined with a mix of mass shootings, terror attacks, natural disasters, technological forebodings and celebrity deaths. Trump can't be blamed for all of this, yet each of those years was widely decried as the "worst year ever." So profound is the sense of relentless decline that an entire genre of cultural commentary has sprung up building off the uneasy feeling that none of this is entirely real. We're living in some sort of parallel universe, a "bizzaroverse," or stub, or alternative timeline in which the joke is on us, the playthings of an alien intelligence. Egged on by Elon Musk, the pothead Falstaff of Silicon Valley, there have even been serious (or at least semi-serious) efforts at trying to figure out whether we're actually living in a simulation.[3]

We (probably) aren't living in a simulation, though it might be more comforting if we were. The disturbing truth is that we've become the oblivious characters in an apocalyptic thriller, so busy with worrying about getting the kids to soccer practise or stressing over what to make for supper that we are missing the forest for the tweets.

* * *

ONE OF THE more salient features of our current moment is how everything seems to be going wrong at the same time.

Again, the 24/7 obsession with Donald Trump was a constant distraction. For his entire term, Trump and his White House served as a catalyst and a cauldron for the seething culture war that has consumed politics in the United States, and which has now spread to countries across the West. But while we've been arguing over weaponized free speech and pronouns and statues of old white guys and the merits, or existence, of cancel culture, the apocalypse montage has been droning away. But unlike in the movies, where it's usually a sudden Big Event that shocks humanity, ours is a slow-moving thing, a relentless secular decline that never quite grows into The Big One, but never really reverses itself either. And this decline is itself masked by what looks to be progress: How can things be getting worse when there's a new season of *The Mandalorian* ready for streaming while you order hipster cheeseburgers for delivery through UberEats or while away the hours on TikTok?

But below deck on the Western techno-consumerist pleasure cruise, all is not well. The economic, political, demographic, environmental, political, and cultural foundations of our civilization are all under enormous stress, and our long-standing failsafe—the essentially rational character of our problem-solving and decision-making—is in crisis.

One of our society's basic assumptions is the idea of steady economic growth. But there is increasing evidence that we're in the midst of what's been called secular stagnation.[4] Having exhausted the big gains from the Industrial Revolution, we're now in a sustained period of long-term slow growth, and it isn't clear how we're going to get out of it.

On the political side, our longstanding faith in the virtues of liberal democracy appears to be coming to an end.[5] The decline of trust in democracy, the rise of anti-liberal convictions and a growing openness to authoritarian rule, especially amongst the young, are widespread in both the emerging democracies of Eastern Europe and the more entrenched democracies of the West. An extreme polarization in society has led to the politicization of virtually everything, with conspiracy theories metastasizing in an information ecosystem that has become entirely unmoored from reality.

Meanwhile, the bill for our exploitative approach to the natural world is finally coming due. Climate change itself is enough to worry about, and it's happening a lot faster than we expected, with parts of California on the verge of becoming virtually uninhabitable. To that we can add a growing antibiotic-resistance crisis, or what some experts have called "an antibiotic apocalypse."[6] Even more frightening, nature itself—the buzzing, blooming plenitude we take for granted—seems to be emptying out. Insects are disappearing,[7] as are animals.[8] The oceans are full of plastic.[9]

And then there's the fact that people have simply stopped having kids. A study from *The Lancet* that came out in the middle of 2020 forecast what it called "jaw dropping" declines in global fertility, with a number of countries, including Spain and Japan, expected to see their populations cut in *half* by the end of the century.[10]

The connection between economic development and a decline in birth rates is well established, and mostly positive, since it's almost always the direct result of the emancipation of women. Women being able to have children on their own terms, with whom they want when they want, is progress no matter how you parse it. But developed countries tend to have lower fertility rates for other reasons as well. With affluence comes greater lifestyle choices and opportunities for work, travel, entertainment, distraction, and excitement. For many people in the developed world, children are seen as more of a buzzkill than a source of fulfilment and joy, and a robust social safety net means that children are less necessary as caregivers for their elderly parents.

One of the most paradoxical aspects of development is that, for people in developed countries, having children can be prohibitively expensive. Kids drive up the cost of housing and require larger automobiles. They cost a lot to feed and clothe and keep entertained. The increasingly high cost of education, especially at the post-secondary level, is forcing students or their parents to take on unsustainable levels of debt. All of this helps explain why one of the most common reasons women give for delaying children, or not having any at all, is that it's too expensive.[11] The paradox resolves itself when you realize just how much of our wealth is devoted to various forms of competitive consumption, status-seeking arms races, and other delusion-induced activities. We're rich, but we spend our money on the wrong things.

What's strange is that our collective response to all of these crises has been to hide from the future and immerse ourselves in the sepia-toned comforts of the past. Like an insect preserved in amber, our culture has become almost completely encased in nostalgia. Whether it's books, movies, or television, popular culture is largely devoted to reboots, revivals, or re-imaginings of pop culture past. The 1980s have gotten particular attention of late (television shows like *Stranger Things* or *Halt and Catch Fire*, movies like *Wonder Woman 1984* or Stephen King's *It* are just few examples out of hundreds), possibly because it was the last decade before the internet arrived and swallowed everything.

Nostalgia has taken over our politics as well. The populist movements that have recently swept through the West, most notably Brexit and Donald Trump's "MAGA" movement, are largely built on a yearning for a dimly remembered past, when things were simpler and politicians more authentic. Instead of building an optimistic future in which our children can live and thrive, we've opted to bury our heads in the past while the world burns.

Maybe some, or even all of this is just temporary, and these trends will reverse themselves. Or perhaps some of our fears are overstated, and we'll figure out solutions to the ones that aren't. Humans are smart and innovative, after all. But what if the opposite is the case? Or what if this is just a partial list and there are actually dozens, if not hundreds of similar patterns or trends or phenomena that we're ignoring or downplaying or simply not seeing?

* * *

THE PLOT OF William Gibson's 2014 novel *The Peripheral* see-saws between a rural American town of the near future and early twenty-second-century London. In-between these two eras was "the jackpot," a thinly described dystopian happening that killed billions of humans. Civilization has been left more or less intact, and at a high level of technological development. The problem is that there's just... less of it. Less nature, fewer people, less everything.

The jackpot happens entirely off-stage; Gibson doesn't give it much exposition and the details are mostly left to the reader's imagination. But as the book makes clear, the jackpot wasn't the result of a single big event: "No comets crashing, nothing you could really call a nuclear war," says one character. "Just everything else, tangled in the changing climate: droughts, water shortages, crop failures ... diseases that were never quite the one big pandemic but big enough to be historic events in themselves."

The jackpot, then, is not an event. It's a process. It's globalization, climate change, pandemics, pesticide use, overfishing, excess packaging, social media, political polarization, and all the rest of it. In various interviews and commentary, Gibson himself has described the jackpot as a civilizational car wreck at least a century in the making. More than anything else, the jackpot is the consequence of humans being humans under the conditions of modernity.

In Gibson's view, our long-term decline is the result of the inevitable working out of the internal logic of our way of life. In the grand scheme of things, Donald Trump's presidency barely registers as an event. This same point is made explicit in *Agency*, the 2020 quasi-sequel to *The Peripheral* that takes place in an alternative timeline or "stub" in which Hillary Clinton has won the 2016 election. While the fictional President Clinton is more competent than the real-world Trump (the novel's plot is driven by an impending nuclear exchange in Turkey that Clinton manages to head off), Gibson makes it clear that this will have no impact on the long-term future of the stub. The jackpot is coming, and mere partisan politics can't affect it one way or another.

This book is, in a sense, an attempt to explain what Gibson's jackpot consists of. The argument is that the patterns of the past few decades are what decline looks like: a punctuated equilibrium of disruption and recovery in which each disruption is a little worse than the previous one, each recovery a little less robust. It isn't the One Big Thing that we've been conditioned by Hollywood to think of as the apocalypse. It's not a massive earthquake or asteroid hitting the Earth or the moon blowing up or an alien arrival. Decline is a bunch of little things that add up: the planet warming, the oceans filling with plastic, our political institutions decaying, the economy stagnating. And the one big backstop we've relied upon for centuries now, the Enlightenment safety net of science, reason, and progress that has helped us confront and solve the problems we've faced, is failing us.

In fact, the ultimate argument of this book is that we are in decline precisely because we have run up against the limits of reason and our capacity to deal with our problems. For all its comforts and pleasures and fascinations, modernity turns out to be its own worst enemy, and the extended period of growth and stability we thought was "normal" turned out to be an aberration. Humanity is in serious trouble, and while it isn't the apocalypse, it might well be the beginning of the end.

But back to the beginning: If we're going to talk about decline, we need to look at whatever happened to progress.

1. On Progress

THERE'S A FAMOUS scene in *Conan the Barbarian*, the 1982 Arnold Schwarzenegger film, where Conan and a few of his Mongol buddies are sitting around a campfire at night shooting the breeze, when out of nowhere the Mongol chief demands to know "what is best in life." One of the Mongols pipes up: "The open steppe, fleet horse, falcons at your wrist, and the wind in your hair." "Wrong!," shouts the chief. He asks the same question of Conan, who comes back with the classic answer: "Crush your enemies, see them driven before you, hear the lamentation of the women." Cheers all around.

It's a great scene. It's also a quick summary of one of the oldest debates in political philosophy over the precise character of the state of nature. The first Mongol takes the side of Jean-Jacques Rousseau, who argued that life in the state of nature is basically good. A man might be solitary, but he is free to pursue his basic needs and desires, and he is happy. In contrast, Conan's view is tribal, dramatic, and violent. In this he's largely channelling Thomas Hobbes, who saw the state of nature as a situation of constant danger and life itself as "solitary, poor, nasty, brutish, and short."

It doesn't take sophisticated political theory or historical anthropology to see that Hobbes hit closer to the mark than Rousseau. Anyone who's ever lived with roommates knows this intuitively. Roommate life, especially in university, is the state of nature writ domestic. The dishes pile up in the sink, the bathroom never gets cleaned, the garbage is never taken out, and everyone ends up shopping and cooking and cleaning for themselves. Bedroom doors are shut, stereos cranked. Factions arise, pettiness abounds, with communal living always on the verge of breaking into open hostilities. Living with university roommates is the closest to raw barbarism most of us will ever experience.

As many scholars have noted, Hobbes' state of nature essentially describes a collective action problem in which a group of individuals would be collectively better off if they were to cooperate, but where they are unable to do so because of the logical structure of their situation. A classic example is the so-called "prisoner's dilemma," which imagines a scenario where two conspirators are arrested and held in separate cells. Each is offered the same deal: If you squeal on your colleague and he keeps quiet, you'll get a short sentence while he gets the book thrown at him. But if you keep quiet and he squeals, the opposite sentencing will result. The optimal situation is thus for both of you to keep quiet and receive moderate sentences. But because of the way the situation is set up, no matter what your colleague does, you're better off squealing.[12]

This is the general structure of all collective action problems, from roommates leaving their dishes in the sink, to the refusal of drivers to "zipper merge" when two lanes go down to one, to the Cold War arms race between the US and the Soviet Union. In every case, the socially optimal scenario is for everyone to cooperate by giving up a small bit of freedom or advantage in exchange for improved group benefit. And yet it's always in each participant's narrow self-interest to defect from the cooperative arrangement, no matter what the other members of the arrangement choose to do. The resulting equilibrium is that everyone ends up worse off than if they cooperated. There are more dishes, more traffic, more nuclear weapons than anyone wants.

The key point is that behaviour that is collectively self-defeating in this way is often privately or individually rational. And this is important, because it means that the problem with the state of nature is not that people hate one another, that they're irrational, or that they're morally misguided. The problem with people in the state of nature is that they are in a position where though it would be collectively optimal, there are numerous obstacles to cooperation. In some cases people don't trust one another enough to cooperate. In other cases, it is difficult to ensure a fair choice between collective goods and private ones: when given a choice between a private good and a poorly funded public good (such as public schools), many will choose the private option, even though, given a proper choice, they would have preferred a well-funded public system.

And that's why actual barbarism is not necessarily characterized by Hobbes' war of all against all—it's not chaos—but rather by a form of small-group tribalism. Cooperation and trust are generated by close family ties and in situations where collective behaviour can be enforced through external sanctions like group pressure or the threat of ostracization or violence by those in charge.

The problem is, tribalism doesn't scale well. Once you get a society of a certain size, informal enforcement mechanisms and external sanctions lose their effectiveness. The path out of barbarism is what we call civilization. The transition to civilization has a number of distinct features, including the growing division of economic labour, the emergence of hierarchy, the stratification of society into social classes, the weakening of familial or tribal ties, and the replacement of force and moral pressure with bureaucracy, public institutions, and the rule of law. At the heart of this process is the expansion of what we can call joint or collective action under a general principle of equality and the rule of law. Which is to say, a group becomes civilized when it gains the ability to engage in large-scale collective action under a common system of laws. As the philosopher John Stuart Mill put it,

> In savage communities each person shifts for himself; except in war (and even then very imperfectly), we seldom see any joint operations carried on by the union of many; nor do savages, in general, find much pleasure in each other's society. Wherever, therefore, we find human beings acting together for common purposes in large bodies, and enjoying the pleasures of social intercourse, we term them civilized.[13]

The name we in the West give to this civilizing process is progress. More concretely, civilization as a form of large-scale political and social cooperation is the basis of progress in all other areas, including arts and letters, science and technology, markets and morals, health and happiness. It's not a stretch to say that the idea of progress is built into the very idea of civilization—progress is simply what a civilization does.

Looking back over the sweep of recorded human history, who would deny that progress has occurred? Pick any metric you like, from life expectancy to wealth to education levels to technological development and things seem to be going pretty well. We are richer, healthier, and more knowledgeable than we've ever been, and we have every reason to believe things will continue this way for a long time to come. Civilization, goes the assumption, is a ratchet of progress, a one-way ride into the future. To vary the metaphor, we have climbed a ladder out of barbarism and kicked it away behind us.

How do we know this? We know it because we have become enlightened.

* * *

THE CLASSIC ENLIGHTENMENT storyline goes something like this: For most of human existence, ignorance had the upper hand as we remained mired in one form of barbarism or another. Life might not have been solitary (even at our most wretched we're a highly social species), but almost everywhere it was poor, nasty, brutish, and short. It was also marked by ignorance, superstition, and prejudice. But sometime around the end of the seventeenth century, science began to fight free of the clerics' grip. Into politics and morals came the ideals of liberty, tolerance, constitutionalism, the separation of church and state—all premised on the idea that *reason* was the ultimate source of legitimacy and authority. Along with this shift toward reason came economic growth, the flowering of knowledge and science, the rejection of faith and dogmatism, and the overthrowing of monarchies, all powered by Immanuel Kant's Enlightenment maxim, "Dare to Know!"

The promise of the Enlightenment project is that it's a package deal, that progress in politics, science, morals, and economics are all fundamentally connected. It's not just that one leads to or enables the other, it's that in many ways they are all just different aspects or implementations of the same thing; namely, the capacity of each individual to use reason and exercise their autonomy.

Even Bertrand Russell, the old sourpuss philosopher who complained that everywhere he looked he saw madness, superstition, nonsense, and other forms of intellectual rubbish (what today we'd call bullshit), was inclined to this view of things. As Russell saw it, the liberal outlook and the scientific outlook were intellectual counterparts in that what defines them is not which opinions are held but how they are held. For both the political liberal and the scientist, beliefs must be held tentatively and undogmatically—a new argument or evidence might at any moment lead to a modification of one's position, or even its abandonment. In this Russell found a mission for philosophy. Where he once believed that the project of philosophy was to discover eternal truths, he now saw it as the logical clarification of thought.[14]

This was not a very cool position, even for 1947; something Russell himself acknowledged. "We have almost reached the point," he wrote, "where praise of rationality is held to mark a man as an old fogey regrettably surviving from a bygone age."[15]

Truth be told, praising reason has almost always been uncool, and the Enlightenment train went off the rails almost as soon as it pulled out of the station. The French Revolution descended into the Terror, not despite its ideals but because of them. And we've been inclined to look askance at reason ever since. Its virtues remain limited, its promise unmet. The nineteenth-century Romantics saw the Enlightenment belief in rationality as something of a cult, which led them to look for the basis of truth elsewhere, such as in nature or the emotions.

But it was the twentieth century that really put reason on the ropes. Shocked by the bureaucratization of mass killing by the Nazis and the escalating alliance between science and arms development that culminated in the atomic bomb, after the Second World War much of the self-described progressive left embraced irrationalism, transformed itself into the "counterculture," and embraced all forms of flakiness from points east and west. Far from helping light the way out of the darkness of barbarism, for much of the left, reason came to be seen as just another way of exercising power, with logic serving as nothing more than a disguised form of oppression.

Today the antipathy to reason is found predominantly (though still not exclusively) on the right. It's hard to say when the shift started and why, but disillusionment with the technocratic dreams of the sixties and the economic stagnation of the seventies surely played a role. Things really changed, though, when Ronald Reagan was elected president in 1980. Reagan's election, combined with the launch of 24/7 cable news (CNN started broadcasting earlier that summer), taught conservatives that short talking points, however tangentially related to the truth, could, through repetition, dominate the news cycle and take hold in the public mind as fact. Today, thanks to George W. Bush-era derision directed at the "reality-based community" and the post-truth/fake-news mantra of Trumpism, for many conservatives professing belief in truth, facts, and evidence amounts to what Canadian conservative prime minister Stephen Harper once sneeringly described as "committing sociology."

Yet despite spending much of the last century intellectually friendless, the Enlightenment has shown signs of getting its mojo back. The past few years have seen, for example, the release of a clutch of books either defending the original Enlightenment or calling for a return to its animating virtues as a way of solving the problems of today. The most significant of these is Steven Pinker's 2018 tome *Enlightenment Now: The Case for Reason, Science, Humanism, and Progress*.[16]

His strategy is to show how the Enlightenment virtues of reason, science, and humanism have contributed to human progress, using pretty much the same approach he used in *Better Angels*; namely, with lots and lots and lots of graphs, charts, and statistics. Pick a metric, any metric: health and wealth, peace and safety, democracy and human rights, education and quality of life—all the lines on all the graphs are pointing in the right direction. We're living longer, healthier lives than our parents and our grandparents, and our children will almost certainly live longer and healthier lives than us. The world is getting richer, with tens of millions more people getting pulled out of poverty with each passing year.

But the important point isn't that Pinker thinks everything is going tickety-boo. He concedes that humanity faces serious problems, most notably from climate change and nuclear proliferation. What he wants to emphasize is that these are manageable problems, *given the proper application of reason*. That is, as long as we keep our heads and remember what got us here in the first place, there are few problems we can't solve if we put our minds to them.

He makes a solid case. It is difficult to conceive how much of a struggle life was not that long ago, but you do get the flavour of it from some of Pinker's graphs showing things such as the decline, over time, in the cost of artificial light. In 1800 in England, you'd have to labour for six hours to pay for an hour's light from a tallow candle; by 1950 you'd need to work for eight seconds for an hour of light from an incandescent bulb, and in 1994 the same hour of light from a compact fluorescent would cost you a half-second's toil.

But if proof of the Enlightenment's merits is what you're looking for, the key document in Pinker's book is a chart showing the change in Gross World Product since the time of Christ. It is effectively a flat line until the year 1800, when it starts to curve sharply upward, with the curve turning into a near vertical line by the beginning of the twentieth century. If that isn't progress, nothing is.

Charts like this suggest that, sometime around the beginning of the eighteenth century, a hurdle was cleared and humanity reached a new, more permanent stage of its growth and evolution. Over the next hundred and fifty years or so, the world became steadily more liberal, more democratic, and more prosperous—it was like we'd climbed a ladder to a new level of development then kicked it away.

The definitive statement of the idea that progress in morals, politics, and economics hangs together as a sort of package deal was made in a short 1989 essay in *The National Interest*—at the time a niche American neocon journal—by Francis Fukuyama. The Soviet Union was clearly on its last legs, but Fukuyama argued that something more than the Cold War seemed to be coming to an end. What Mikhail Gorbachev's twin reforms of *glasnost* (political openness) and *perestroika* (economic restructuring) signified, according to Fukuyama, was nothing less than the "unabashed victory of economic and political liberalism." He argued that the relentless extension of Western forms of consumer capitalism, combined with the absence of any systematic alternative to liberalism, had led to a single possible conclusion: the triumph of the West and the end of "History" as such. As Fukuyama put it, we had reached "the end point of mankind's ideological evolution and the universalization of Western liberal democracy as the final form of human government."

Key to Fukuyama's argument is the notion that societies don't suddenly become liberal, it's that they stop pretending to have a higher ideology. In other words, the terms in which they describe their ambitions sound liberal. Authoritarians and nationalists, for instance, might try to cloak their actions in a veneer of democratic legitimacy. This, more than anything, suggests that in liberal democracy human civilization has reached the universal and homogeneous state, a form of social organization that will be liberal and democratic in the political realm, and supported and fostered by a free-market-driven consumer culture. In his 1989 essay, Fukuyama summarized the universal and homogeneous state as "liberal democracy in the political sphere combined with easy access to vcrs and stereos in the economic." Netflix and iPhones for all.

The end-of-history thesis was always contentious, but by 2008 it was completely untenable, as old school strongmen started flexing their pecs in South Asia (Musharraf in Pakistan), Africa (notably Mugabe in Zimbabwe), and South America (Chavez). Punctuating it all was Russia's invasion of Georgia, which even Fukuyama acknowledged seemed to mark what he called a "new phase" in global geopolitics.[17] Compounding this growing geopolitical unrest was the global financial crisis of 2008, which proved a major catalyst for everything to come: the growth of inequality, the rise of populism and right-wing nationalism, the retrenchment of democracy, the political shocks of Brexit and the 2016 election of Donald Trump as president of the United States.

It's important to be clear about the problem. It's not just that countries such as China and Russia are now challenging the United States and its erstwhile allies in the West for dominance in an increasingly Hobbesian international order. It's that there's little evidence that the leadership of either country feels obliged to pay the slightest lip service to the virtues of liberal democracy and global capitalism. China in particular is defiantly illiberal, given to describing ideals such as the rule of law as a quaint Western fetish.

If anything, it is in the United States, and in many of the seemingly entrenched democracies of the West, where

liberalism is on the run, democracy is in retreat, and capitalism is in question. In place of these things we're getting
right-wing populism, identity politics, and protectionism,
and these are not merely features of an "incomplete" transition to liberalism. Things are going in the wrong
direction even in the countries where it seemed like history had most resoundingly come to an end.

So what happened? Our mistake was believing that the
world had figured things out in a way that was more or
less stable and permanent. It turns out that it was this
period of stability and growth that was temporary. Progress itself was something that fed off a massive one-time
windfall we gained access to in the nineteenth century.
We didn't climb a ladder, we stumbled into a buffet. We've
been feasting off that buffet for a few centuries now.
Unfortunately, it looks like the party is coming to an end.

2. On Stagnation

ON MAY 30, 2020, space travel history was made when a rocket lifted off from the famous Launch Complex 39A at NASA's Kennedy Space Center in Florida. Was it a manned mission to Mars? The testing of a completely new form of propulsion? The first step toward what would become a permanent base on the moon?

Not quite. A NASA administrator marked the moment with some solemn words: "Today a new era in human spaceflight begins as we once again launched American astronauts on American rockets from American soil on their way to the International Space Station."[18]

American rockets have been putting American astronauts into space since 1961. The ISS was launched in 1998 and has been continuously inhabited for over twenty years. What made this event so groundbreaking was that it was a rocket built by SpaceX, and the first time a private company had launched American astronauts into orbit. And while NASA didn't dwell on it, it was also the first time Americans had put Americans into space since the Space Shuttle program was shut down in

2011. The US had been relying on rides from the Russians ever since.

This would shock anyone who'd been doing a Rip Van Winkle since the early 1970s. Everyone knows the key lines from the most famous speech about space exploration ever delivered. It was September 1962, and President Kennedy was trying to drum up support for the Apollo program, which was America's mission to put a man on the moon. At the time, the United States was in a bit of a funk, with the Soviets appearing to be a step ahead of them at almost every turn. They were making mischief for the Americans in Vietnam, while the Bay of Pigs fiasco hung over Kennedy's presidency like a bad smell. But the Soviets' most notable lead was in space, where they were the first to put a satellite in orbit, the first to put an animal in space, the first to put animals in orbit and return them safely to Earth, and, with Yuri Gagarin, the first to put a man in orbit around the Earth.

Kennedy was looking for something to establish America's undeniable superiority over the Soviets, to underscore the virtues of the country's economy and ingenuity. His advisers told him that the only realistic shot they had of beating the USSR was in landing a man on the moon. It was a stretch goal for sure, a difficult and hugely expensive undertaking. But in 1961 Kennedy got Congressional approval for the funds to land a man on the moon before the decade was out.

The American people, however, were slow to catch on to the drama and urgency of the race to the moon, so a year later, Kennedy stood before a crowd at Rice Stadium in Houston and made his case. After some throat clearing and a bit of a joking around, he got to the nub of it:

We choose to go to the Moon. We choose to go to
the Moon in this decade and do the other things,
not because they are easy, but because they are
hard; because that goal will serve to organize and
measure the best of our energies and skills, because
that challenge is one that we are willing to accept,
one we are unwilling to postpone, and one we
intend to win, and the others, too…[19]

For all its familiarity, this remains stirring stuff. But in
many ways Kennedy's argument for going to the moon
was just a rocket-fuelled version of George Mallory's quip
about why he wanted to climb Mount Everest: "Because
it's there." The moon mission also had a more direct geopolitical dimension, which Kennedy made clear a year
earlier in a much less well-known speech to Congress.
Space was just one very public front in the ongoing battle
between freedom and tyranny.

Kennedy told Congress, "We go to space because whatever mankind must undertake, free men must share." He
went on to demand that Congress either commit fully to
the moon, or not bother committing at all. It would be
better not to try than to start and then back away. And it
wasn't just Congress that had to commit. The US would
certainly fail unless every person involved—every scientist, engineer, contractor, and public servant—gave "his
personal pledge that this nation will move forward with the
full speed of freedom, in the exciting adventure of space."[20]

The full speed of freedom. In that simple and remarkable
phrase Kennedy brought together a number of tightly
connected ideas that mortared the fundamental relationship between democracy, capitalism, and innovation. It

wasn't really about the moon—as Kennedy freely admitted, he didn't actually care about space as such. It was just that doing hard things, and solving hard problems, is what free people do. They don't submit to authority, they commit to collective action. In doing so, they unleash "the full speed of freedom."

Sixty years after Kennedy's speech to Congress, you'd be hard pressed to find anyone willing to make the case that accomplishing hard tasks, solving hard problems, committing to collective action, is a particular ambition or ideal or expertise of democracy.

So the return to space with SpaceX is good news by one measure. But by most other measures, it marks a rather surprising stagnation. Fifty years before the SpaceX success, Apollo 11 and Apollo 12 had already landed astronauts on the moon, and the crew of Apollo 13 had been brought safely back to Earth after an oxygen tank exploded, threatening the lives of the crew. With at least four more Apollo missions underway, if you'd been put into cryogenic storage for a half-century nap on May 30, 1970, you could reasonably have expected to wake up to some version of the spacefaring society depicted in *2001: A Space Odyssey*. It would have been shocking to find instead that no human had been out of low Earth orbit since 1972, and that NASA had gone nearly a decade without putting anyone into any orbit at all.

It's tempting to think of this stagnation as a specific feature of the space race, but the pattern holds more generally. Compared to the amazing pace of invention and discovery that was the norm from the late 1700s until the first half of the twentieth century, the last fifty years have been a bit of a snooze.

To give a quick run-through: The period from 1770 to
1820 saw the invention of the cotton gin, the electric battery, the steam locomotive, and the Watt engine. If you
entered your fifty-year cryogenic sleep in 1820, you'd have
woken up to a planet transformed by cement, the telegraph, the typewriter, cameras, bicycles, antiseptics,
pasteurization, and dynamite. If you fell back asleep for
another half century, you'd wake up to an entirely different world filled with telephones, movies, electricity,
motorcars, airplanes, machine guns, air conditions, vac-
uums, radio, and radar. And if you embarked on another
fifty-year sleep in 1920, you'd miss the development of jet
planes, space flight, lunar landings, nuclear weapons,
nuclear power, penicillin, electric guitars, vcrs, comput-
ers, video games, the internet, and just about any other
mod con you can imagine.

For two hundred years, every half century of sleep
would have you waking up to a new age of miracle and
wonder: new technologies, stunning advances in health,
wealth, and comfort, amazing new products and consumer goods, and a world steadily shrinking thanks to
new forms of transportation and communication. Politically, things would keep changing enormously as well,
the age of monarchy, colonialism, and empire giving way
to a world order focused on nation states and led by an
ever-growing alliance of liberal democracies.

And then in 2020 you'd wake up maybe a little disap-
pointed. At first it might seem that economic growth had
once again worked its magic; in particular, in the way
everyone was carrying the world's entire cultural inheritance in their pockets. But that would just be the logic of
networked computing (which already existed) playing

itself out. Aside from that, the world would look, in many respects, like things had stalled or even gone backwards.

It wouldn't be just an illusion. Since the 1970s, real wages have seen little to no growth, especially for middle- and low-income earners, while public goods like education and health care are more expensive than ever. Our infrastructure is crumbling, traffic congestion gets worse and worse, our airports are decrepit, and the trains almost never run on time. Nuclear energy, once hailed as the energy of the future, has been a flop. Domestically, there have been huge advances in consumer electronics, like enormous flat-screen televisions and AI-driven sound systems that will play any song you like, all you have to do is ask. But in the realm of the kitchen or the laundry room, there has been a reversal. Dishwashers are slower today than they were forty years ago, hold fewer dishes, and don't get them as clean. Ditto for clothes washers. We're spinning our wheels, and have been for a few decades now.

Narratives that see a widespread economic and tech- nological stagnation settling in sometime around the mid-1970s have become fairly common. And it's pretty clear that the 1970s were some sort of inflection point, a time when we fell off established income, innovation, and progress curves on a number of fronts. The big ques- tion is why?

* * *

THE IDEA OF what economists call "secular stagnation" has been around since the 1930s, when it was popularized by Alvin Hansen, who was a disciple of Keynes. Hansen argued that the combination of an aging population, low rates of immigration, and the exhaustion of technological progress would lead to an imbalance between excess household savings and inadequate business investment. The result would be an extended period of little to no economic growth. The theory has always been controversial, but it got new traction in the aftermath of the economic crisis of 2008, thanks to the Harvard economist Larry Summers. As he saw it, the main reason the economy struggled to recover from the Great Recession was secular stagnation for the precise reasons Hanson gave, namely, an increased propensity to save and a decreased propensity to invest leading to "shortfalls in demand and stunted growth." Summers suggested a number of reasons for why this was happening, including the rich getting richer, an aging population and uncertainty over the length of retirement, and slower growth in the labour force. To get the economy rolling again, he prescribed a form of Keynesianism: governments just needed to spend a lot of money to help spur demand.[21]

But there's a version of the stagnation thesis that's a bit more complicated. In 2011, the economist Tyler Cowen wrote a very influential essay called "The Great Stagnation"[22] in which he argued that the causes of the economic crisis went a lot deeper than the mix of high household debt, overleveraged home ownership, and novel financial instruments such as subprime loans that had become central to the accepted narrative about why the crisis happened. As he saw it, the real problem was something much more profound—the result of basic structural problems with our social and economic systems. According to Cowen, the story began back in the 1970s, when median wages effectively stopped rising, and carried on through the first decade of the new century, which saw virtually no net job creation. Through all this we maintained the illusion of growing prosperity, thanks to increasing household debt and inflated home prices. But, he writes, "All of these problems have a single, little-noticed root cause... We have been living off low-hanging fruit for at least 300 years. We have built social and economic institutions on the expectation of a lot of low-hanging fruit, but that fruit is mostly gone."[23]

What did this bounty consist of? Cowen suggests three possibilities: the benefits of "free land" (which he concedes was land largely stolen from the original occupants), the technological breakthroughs of the Industrial Revolution, and the enormous pool of smart but uneducated people who gradually moved off the farm, into cities, and got educated. Other possible factors include access to cheap and abundant energy sources, especially oil; the expansion of democracy and liberal values; and the slow but steady emancipation of women and their incorporation into the workforce. We have exploited each of these in turn, and each has given us enormous economic gains at very low cost.

Most notably, the Industrial Revolution that transformed Europe in the late-eighteenth century led to an explosion of technological breakthroughs a century later. While the telegraph, railroads, and steam shipping were already around, the period between 1880 and 1940 brought us indoor plumbing, electric lighting, cars, airplanes, the telephone, radio, pharmaceuticals, and plenty of other innovations. Each of these things is near-miraculous on its own, but the real benefits came from combining them:

complicated machines with the cheap and abundant
energy produced by fossil fuels or electricity, say. Add in
fast and increasingly cheap communications, from the telegraph to the radio to the telephone, and ideas can spread
quicker than ever before. The result was the rapid expansion of civilization and progress.

All of this amounts to a pretty stiff counter to the naive
Enlightenment position that progress occurred when we
emerged from our intellectual infancy. According to the
stagnation thesis, what we'd thought of as "progress"
wasn't really a ladder that we climbed to a more permanent plateau of development. It was more like an oasis
that we stumbled upon after wandering around a desert
for millennia.

Still, Tyler Cowen himself remains fairly optimistic.
While the easy pickings are largely gone and it isn't obvious where our next cheap meal is going to come from, he
thinks the situation will probably sort itself out in a couple of decades or so, once we figure out how to realize
significant productivity gains from sources like biotechnology and the internet.[24] There's a more pessimistic
version of the argument, though, that says the root of the
problem isn't just the exhaustion of natural resources or
us hitting up against some technological barriers. Instead,
the causes of the Great Stagnation are fundamentally
political and cultural—and those forces holding back
progress are getting more entrenched, not less.

* * *

ALONG WITH "WE were promised jetpacks!," the "where's
my flying car?" complaint is the go-to refrain of the disaf-

fected hipster futurist. It's also become shorthand for describing the Great Stagnation and the failed promise of futures past. So why don't we have flying cars or jetpacks?

The usual explanation is that hoping for flying cars or jetpacks (or moving sidewalks or tubes that shoot people at high velocity through the downtown core) is a matter of looking for progress in the wrong place. By the middle of the twentieth century, we'd already used up most of the technological headroom available at the level of mechanical development. Flying cars are certainly possible (indeed, many working versions have been built over the years) but they're always some combination of too complicated, too expensive, and too dangerous to make them commercially viable. But that doesn't mean progress stopped happening. The future arrived, just in a different form than we expected. Instead of electro-mechanical forms of transportation, we turned our attention and energies to a space where there was a lot more headroom; namely, information technology and networked computing.

There's certainly something to the idea that, by the 1970s, we'd started to bump against the ceiling of what was possible from the standpoint of mechanical engineering. In the case of the Apollo program, NASA was pushing the limits of existing tech so much that the space suits the astronauts wore on the moon were hand sewn by seamstresses. They were hired for their ability to sew the fabric, a fiberglass-like material called Beta cloth, to the tolerances needed to keep the astronauts alive on the lunar surface. More amazingly, the Apollo guidance computer used a form of ROM called "rope core memory," where each bit of information was encoded by thin wires threaded through tiny, donut-shaped magnetic cores. The bits were threaded by hand, again by seamstresses hired for their care and accuracy. This memory was only ever used in the Apollo guidance computer—it was soon made obsolete by semiconductors.

In many ways, Apollo was an artisanal space program that pushed the absolute limits of what could be done with existing technology. And it's tempting to generalize this example to the Great Stagnation as a whole—by the 1970s, maybe we'd just run out of things we could do with a needle and thread.

But there's another version of the story that sees the problem as essentially political, not technological. In a self-published 2017 book entitled (naturally) *Where's My Flying Car?*, the computer scientist and nanotech futurist J. Storrs Hall argues that The Great Stagnation is real, but that it isn't what most people think it is. The real enemy of progress isn't technological limits but political interference and cultural hostility to science.

The spine of his argument is the story of the rise and fall of the flying car. As Hall argues, there was a healthy R&D industry around the flying car as early as the 1920s. In the natural evolution of things, we should have had affordable, consumer-focused flying cars by the 1970s or '80s. What stopped it was a combination of the bureaucratization of science research, the rise of the regulatory state, and the baleful influence of the luddite wing of the counterculture.

Hall's book has become something of a cult classic amongst engineers, economists, and Silicon Valley types. If you read it, you'll probably learn more than you need to know about flight mechanics, turbine power curves, and rotary wing lift loads. But the story Hall tells about the flying car is just a microcosmic explanation for the more general technological stagnation of the past fifty years. As Hall points out, the Great Stagnation arrived in lockstep with the explosion in PhDs and the large-scale takeover of research and development funding by the state. The result is what he calls "The Machiavelli effect," where centralized funding creates an intellectual elite of political insiders who gain control of a field. This elite have a vested interest in the status quo, which they preserve by controlling access to funding, but also by manipulating the regulatory process to which they have privileged access. For example, he notes that when the Clinton government in the US launched a nanotechnology initiative that redirected existing funding streams, the affected researchers' response was to to re-describe whatever they were already doing as "nanotech."[25] It's a pattern anyone familiar with the Canadian government's recent investments in AI research will recognize.

This sort of turf-protection isn't restricted to science and technology. It's a standard feature of almost any government-funded bureaucracy, including for arts and culture. For anyone who works in Canada's culture industry, the Machiavelli effect is a perfect description of what it's like navigating the funding gatekeepers. The point, which Hall is careful to emphasize, is that there's no conspiracy at work here, just the entirely predictable protection of their interests by people who've done very well under an existing system.

There's a lot going on in Hall's book. It's long and in places pretty technical. It's poorly organized, and he

doesn't always try as hard as he might to separate correlation from causation. For example, he may be right in
claiming that the fantastic potential of nanotechnology,
the basic principles of which have been known since the
1960s, has been sandbagged by a tremendous failure of
imagination. But is it really the case that, if we'd only
been a bit bolder in our ambitions, we'd be on the verge
of being able to replace the entire capital stock of North
America by rebuilding every road, railway, office tower,
and power plant at the submolecular level *in about a
week?* As the kids say, your mileage may vary.

To grasp the force of Hall's central claim, you don't
need a graph showing how the Great Stagnation happened to coincide with a sharp rise in the number of
PhDs awarded each year, nor do you need to believe that
promising research into cold fusion was choked off by
protectionist elements in the physics community. All you
have to do is live in North America in the twenty-first
century, where the basic elements of Hall's story—progress and innovation being stymied by political forces—are
staring us in the face. Canada in particular has become
notorious as a place where it's almost impossible for governments, or even the private sector, to do anything. As
one national columnist put it a few years ago, when yet
another pipeline project was abandoned over ongoing
regulatory uncertainty: Canada has become a place where
"large and controversial projects designed to achieve legal
ends for legitimate businesses *somehow never seem to end
up getting built*" (emphasis in the original).[26]

If anything, the problem is worse in the United States.
Francis Fukuyama, who has in recent years turned his
attention to the question of institutional decay and polit-

ical decline, coined the term "vetocracy" to describe the system of entrenched political interests that have made it very hard to get anything built or done in America. What this amounts to is our old foe, the collective action problem, where any one of an enormous number of interest groups—political, bureaucratic, scientific, corporate, environmental, you name it—has the power to stall or stymie things that are collectively beneficial but not in their narrow self-interest.

So forget flying cars. Why is there no nanotech industry to speak of? Why was the nuclear power industry effectively smothered in the 1970s? Why did the market for general aviation aircraft fall off a cliff in the early 1980s? Why has "cost disease" afflicted so many industries, from education to health care to construction? Why does a mile of subway in New York or London or Toronto cost more than double (in constant dollars) what it cost in the sixties and seventies?[27] Why are trains in the US and Canada significantly slower today than they were a century ago?

The answers to all of these questions have less to do with inherent technological limits and more to do with decaying infrastructure, politics, bureaucracy, and regulation. As Hall puts it, "the trees of knowledge are growing higher than ever, but someone appears to have been spraying paraquat on the low-hanging fruit." The Great Stagnation is more like the great "strangulation." To vary the metaphor, it's like we stumbled out of the desert into a great buffet, ate all the food, and then spent the next forty years tying the chefs up with ever-more stringent rules over what they could cook, under what conditions, and who they could serve it to.

The full speed of freedom is a clarion call from another era. Where democracy, technology, and progress were once aligned and facing full-on toward the future, today democracy is in retreat, technology is stagnating, progress is a dirty word. Politics is eating the world and we have become a culture obsessed with the past.

3. On Politics

THE SATIRICAL WEBSITE *The Onion* once ran a story with the headline: "U.S. Dept. Of Retro Warns: 'We May Be Running Out Of Past." The conceit was that "retro consumption"—that is, the open-pit mining of our pop-cultural past—was creeping ever closer to the present. Where kids in the eighties held fifties-themed dance parties, by the mid-nineties people were already waxing nostalgic for the halcyon days of late-eighties hair metal. The story's (fake) source commented that: "This rapidly shrinking gap between retro and the present day is like a noose closing ever tighter around the neck of American kitsch." First published in 1997, the piece predicted that we'd be "out of past" to romanticize by 2005: "For the first time in history, a phenomenon and nostalgia for that particular phenomenon will actually meet."

They were only off by about five years, the past decade having seen the culmination of what's been called "nostalgia for the present"—the framing and romanticizing of an event or era even as it's occurring. The *Onion* article wasn't so much satire as an incredibly prescient take on how our culture would evolve under the enormous selection pressures of digital media. It's almost impossible to distinguish a nostalgia craze from a consumer craze anymore. Nostalgia is a form of consumerism, and consumerism is now little more than the dip of a credit card into the river of nostalgia that runs through our social media feeds.

As it evolves into the dominant mood of the twenty-first century, nostalgia culture has just become the culture, one where consumer crazes and social media shivers amount to little more than the context-free curation of the past. From this perspective, our obsession with nostalgia is just the flip side of the ideology-free eternal present of the end of history. Unmoored and disconnected from how history has actually unfolded, everything from Victorian-era motifs to Cold War symbolism to survivalist masculine posturing all gets funnelled into the pop-cultural maw, from which it later emerges as one facet or another of contemporary popular culture.

At one level, the current obsession with nostalgia can be read as a straightforward response to rapid technological change. The world is crazy, fast-paced, and fragmented. Our every moment is a flood of texts and DMs and TikTok videos and memes, all of which pass by in an endless stream, seemingly without connection to anything but the passing show.

But this nostalgia-on-demand also points to an even more powerful force driving the cultural moment, which is nostalgia as the principle *product* of our most popular technologies. Video game nostalgia and retro consoles are a huge market. Remember Pokémon Go, the insanely popular app-based game from 2015 that saw crowds of civilians wandering the streets, stumbling into dead bodies, into crime traps, and even to their deaths? Its initial appeal leaned heavily on the nostalgia for the original Game Boy version of Pokémon, which, for many, was one of the first video games they'd loved as kids. There are countless other websites devoted to the curation of the past, including the straightforwardly named Nostalgia Machine, where you enter a given year and get served up a screen populated with links to the Billboard hits of time.[28]

And then there's social media. Facebook has its "On This Day" feature, Twitter has a function that lets you see how your timeline looked any number of years earlier, while Instagram has at-the-ready filters to give any pic the look of a Polaroid that's been fading in a photo album for decades. If you're careless enough to upload your phone's pictures to a cloud service like Google Photos, you'll get a daily nostalgia montage of photos you took on this date one, two, three, and four years ago. You can now spend your days wallowing in the past; indeed, many of us do. Our culture has become a form of nostalgia-as-service. We're forever trapped in our online world, going round and round on an all-encompassing digital version of Don Draper's famous carousel from *Mad Men*.

Some psychologists see this as a good thing, since nostalgia can serve as emotional ballast by keeping us grounded in something certain. Where nostalgia was once seen as a malady, a mental illness to be cured, it's now being interpreted as a healthy corrective to the fast pace of the modern world. The new wisdom is that nostalgia can serve as a cultural security blanket, offering a quantum of comfort or happiness in a world gone crazy.[29]

Missed in all this is the essence of the nostalgic mood, which is not so much about "remembering" but

mis-remembering. Nostalgia only works when we deliberately ignore certain aspects of the past and deliberately
foreground other elements. It's about seeing the past in
a very specific way—as more innocent, naive, and
authentic than the present. All nostalgia is therefore fundamentally about our present feelings of disquiet or
unhappiness, a state that always compares poorly with
the past. And as harmless and inward as that might seem,
it actually has enormous political implications. Under-
neath nostalgia's happy-go-lucky veneer is something a lot
darker: identity politics, populism, and the culture wars.

* * *

ACROSS THE WEST, politics in the twenty-first century has
been dominated by two features: nostalgia-based populism and identity politics. Not only has liberal democracy,
with its pleasant mix of consumer culture and rights-
based individualism, failed to triumph, in many places
it's in retreat, while the hope for a technocratic political
culture based on reason, science, and expertise is
increasingly forlorn.

Almost from the moment he took power in 1999 in
Russia, Vladimir Putin started building an autocracy on a
profound sense of national loss over the demise of the
Soviet Union, which he once called "the greatest political
catastrophe of the 20th century." A decade later in the
United States, one of the first and clearest politics-as-nos-
talgia plays was the so-called Tea Party revolution—the
political movement that began in 2010 as a sort of reactionary insurgency within the Republican party in the
United States. More recently, the politics of nostalgia has

been the driving force behind two of the most seismic events of the last half-decade; namely, the election of Donald Trump as president of the United States, and the success of the Leave faction in the Brexit vote of 2016. Nostalgia has also been seen as a motivator behind other recent Western populist movements, including in Turkey, Hungary, Poland, and Brazil.

At first blush there seems to be no obvious connection between the nostalgic attraction of pop culture and political movements like Brexit or Trump's MAGA agenda. After all, there's nothing inherently political about, say, digging out your old flannel shirt and spinning a Nirvana CD. One might wonder, too, what harm there is in grownups bonding over a few rounds of Pokémon Go.

But this objection ignores the ways in which popular culture and politics have always intersected, each at once reflecting and responding to the other. It's surely no accident, for example, that television shows like *Downton Abbey* and *The Crown* romanticize a distinctive British culture and thus help normalize the political drivers of Brexit. Or take a television show like Netflix's enormously popular *Stranger Things*, with its racially diverse cast of Dungeons and Dragons nerds. Here, a veneer of current diversity politics helps distract us from the fact that the popular culture the show celebrates was, by current standards, enormously racist and misogynist. It's can be difficult to notice just how much these seemingly innocuous exercises in cultural nostalgia feed into populist fantasies about a lost golden age.

The main features of this populism are by now familiar: the rejection of science and other forms of expertise, hostility towards immigrants, hatred of the mainstream media, and a deep antagonism towards elites of all stripes. The animating core of populism is the notion that a pure, true, authentic tribe or "people" are at every turn being subjugated, insulted, denigrated, and exploited by a class of globalist and cosmopolitan elites.

The narrative of an authentic folk betrayed by a false elite has fuelled a reactionary conservative agenda, to the point where the predominant form of conservatism that exists in many Western countries is the populist version. Mainstream conservatives do exist, in academia, think tanks, and the media. There's also a substantial cottage industry of writings devoted to wooing conservatism back to its roots in small government economics and libertarian politics. The wooers haven't had much success though, and there's little reason to think this will change any time soon.

In its rejection of reason, science, and expertise, the right was to a large extent just picking up the baton from a left that spent much of the twentieth century warning of an unholy alliance between science, technology, bureaucracy, and capitalism. Long before the Tea Party or the election of Donald Trump or the Brexit vote or any other manifestation of contemporary populism, the table was set for an across-the-board crisis of liberalism. In the West both the left and right have harboured a decades-in-the-making hostility to the status quo, a sense that the game is rigged, and that the solution to this problem is to be found in some combination of emotion, unreason, and identity politics. The inevitable consequence is a culture war.

Every culture war rests on the shared conviction that the key to political power is control over the culture. In purest form, the ideology underpinning any culture war is the belief that all politics boils down to cultural politics; everything else, including control over the economy or various political institutions, is epiphenomenal. All politics is a winner-take-all struggle over whose taste, and which values, should dominate.

The culture war that most people are familiar with (so familiar that many people don't even recognize it as a culture war) is the one that's been raging in the West, more or less continuously since the 1960s, between the establishment and the counterculture. In a nutshell, the countercultural idea was based on a critique of "mass society," which holds that society is a set of interlocking and self-reinforcing systems, institutions, and ideals that promote and enforce the conformity that capitalism requires in order to function properly. From religion to schools to the medical establishment to the mass media and advertising, our culture is one big system of repression. From a political-activist perspective, you resist this system by "jamming" the culture by behaving in non-conformist ways.

This was the philosophical basis underlying the original sex, drugs, and rock and roll ideals of the counterculture: If society wants you to get married and have kids and live in the suburbs, you resist by having a lot of free sex and living in a commune. If The Man wants you to wear a suit and tie and keep your hair short, you resist by wearing bell bottoms and a tie-dye shirt and growing your hair long. And while the specific moves or poses changed over the decades, the basic structure of countercultural rebellion remained constant through successive movements, such as punk in the seventies and grunge in the nineties, culminating in the anti-consumerism movement of the early 2000s.[30]

While the counterculture—along with its cultural off-shoots such as "cool," "alternative," "edgy," and "hip"—has pretty much faded out as a serious political battlefront, it remains important for a couple of reasons. First, it established the idea that a culture war was, on the one hand, always and everywhere a battle between the forces of repression and conformity and those of freedom and individualism. On the other, it helped cement the conviction that counterculture was an essentially left-wing phenomenon, and that the forces of conformity were arrayed on the right.

This dynamic, of a fundamental conflict between a non-conformist countercultural left and a repressive establishment right, came to a head during the last great culture war of the late '80s and early '90s. An early salvo was Allan Bloom's bestselling 1987 book *The Closing of the American Mind*, which blamed the counterculture-infused liberalism of students and the academy (as well as, of all people, Mick Jagger) for their embrace of cultural relativism and political nihilism.

Bloom's book sparked an enormous debate about the relationship between popular culture and political values, as well as the proper role of universities, the curriculum, and the so-called Western Canon. Five years later, the American paleoconservative Pat Buchanan gave a name to this debate during a stump speech for the re-election of President George H W Bush. Drawing an explicit comparison to America's still-fresh victory over communism, Buchanan said: "There is a religious war going on in this country. It is a cultural war, as critical to the kind of nation we shall be as was the Cold War itself, for this war is for the soul of America."[31] According to Buchanan, the

Baby Boomer, liberal, post-hippie Clintons were on one side of this war, George H W Bush and the God-fearing people of small-town America on the other.

Bill Clinton won the election of course, and his victory helped reinforce the view that, in America at least, conservatism was the party of religiosity, conformity, and establishment values, while the liberal "I didn't inhale" left was just the respectable face of the counterculture. It also reinforced bipartisan convictions around the importance of the culture war itself: both sides knew that controlling the culture was the key to political power; it just so happened that the liberals had won for a change.

This historical alliance between countercultural politics and the left is so entrenched that it's hard to remember that they are logically distinct; that there's nothing natural about connecting the two. In fact, what makes the present culture war so confusing, and so remarkable, is how its defining characteristic is the wholesale migration of countercultural thinking from left to right.

This was no accident; rather, it was an explicit strategy devised by Steve Bannon, Donald Trump's former campaign manager and chief of staff. Bannon's analysis of the overall political situation in America, and the respecttive strategies pursued by the left and the right, was in most respects completely orthodox, in that he saw political power as belonging to whoever controlled the culture. Indeed, despite long-standing Republican dominance in Washington, Bannon believed that in choosing to pursue cultural politics, the left had in fact adopted the better strategy. "While we were taking over Washington," he said, "the liberals were busy taking over Hollywood." In other words, the right controlled the state, but the left controlled the far more powerful instruments of cultural production. "Politics is downstream from culture" was Bannon's preferred slogan for the phenomenon he'd identified: the culture had become so hostile to right-wing ideas that it was seriously limiting conservatives' ability manoeuver politically. In order to reclaim territory lost to the left, Bannon decided, the right needed to adopt a new cultural politics.[32]

The need for a new "cultural politics" is what ultimately gave rise to the idea of the alt-right. What's often been missed in the debate over alt-right politics is that it is essentially a countercultural movement with a right-wing instead of left-wing valence.[33] What makes the alt-right a countercultural phenomenon is that it has internalized the essential feature of the counterculture: the celebration of rule-breaking or norm-violation in whatever form. What makes it a conservative phenomenon is that the rules or norms of collective action or conformity that it seeks to undermine are those championed by the left under the guise of political correctness.

The alt-right's nonconformist gambits run from the refusal to be "politically correct" (e.g., objecting to using the preferred pronouns of trans individuals) to the ubiquitous online use of racist and misogynistic language, from the embrace of Nazi tropes and symbols to the rejection of virtually all forms of expertise and authority and even the repudiation of the legitimacy of the state and the rule of law. In general, whenever a norm or rule is designed to facilitate collective action in the name of progress, the alt-right sees itself as dutybound to violate it. Dissent is seen as an intrinsically political act.

It is amazing to consider the extent to which this is a repudiation of the conservative position in the culture war of the late '80s and early '90s, marking, as it does, a complete reversal of the traditional positions of left and right. The norm-flouting nihilism of the alt-right has been met, on the left, with the obsessive imposition of a constellation of increasingly strict and constantly shifting rules about people's public language and behaviour. This behaviour is what goes by the general term "woke politics," but a more apt term might be to call it the "ctrl-left."

It's important to underscore how unexpected this development is. For well over half a century, it's been an article of faith, agreed to by all sides, that the right was the side of rules, order, tradition, and circumspection, while the left was the party of rebellion, individualism, freedom, and transgression. Now the political valences have reversed themselves, with the right setting itself up as the true countercultural opposition to the left's restrictiveness and enforced conformity.

This has given rise to a predictable dynamic, with each side being pushed into an increasingly polarized and extreme set of positions and behaviours. On the right, you get what's been called the "weaponization" of free speech, where the cultural norms and legal protections around free expression are exploited for ulterior motives. "Free speech" becomes at best a fig leaf for bad faith; or worse, an opportunity to incite opposition, hatred, and violence.[34]

A common tactic is for right-wing groups to take advantage of the fact that universities or public libraries often allow their spaces to be booked by the public for meetings and events. They then invite notorious figures or hate-mongers to speak, knowing full well that it will cause outrage in the community, which they then take advantage of to gain publicity, public sympathy, or to fundraise. The actual talk or presentation itself is of no consequence. Examples of this gambit abound. Ann Coulter and the now-disgraced Milo Yiannopoulos both had scheduled talks cancelled by UC Berkeley in early 2017. Later that same year, activists forced Toronto's Ryerson University to cancel a planned panel discussion about free speech on campus, which was to feature the academic Jordan Peterson and the right-wing journalist Faith Goldy.

At the far side of the spectrum sits the form of woke politics known as "cancel culture," in which someone is browbeaten or mobbed out of their social circles or professional life because of things they have said or done that are deemed "problematic." Being cancelled is essentially a modern form of shaming or ostracism that is typically catalyzed and amplified through social media. Those who defend the practice like to say that cancel culture doesn't exist, that it's merely a form of "consequence culture." After all (goes the argument), the right to free speech doesn't guarantee the right to be free of consequences, and if your employer sees fit to fire you for something you tweeted, well, whose fault is that?[35]

It should be obvious that there's a symbiotic relationship between these two positions: the weaponization of free speech is a reaction to the politically correct diktats of woke politics, and cancel culture is a counter-reaction to the weaponization of free speech by the alt-right. (This dynamic is clearly at work in the Ryerson University example mentioned above). Both positions share two other characteristics worth noting: an enormous amount of bad faith, and a perversion of the original (and largely positive) social norms surrounding free speech on the one hand, and political correctness on the other.

Third, it is worth noting that they are both fundamentally *performative* exercises, in which the ultimate goal isn't to exchange ideas, engage in public debate or deliberation, or improve relations in the workplace, but to gain attention, incite a mob, attract followers. In the end, both the alt-right and ctrl-left are interested in one thing above all: to accelerate and entrench the polarizing in-group/out-group tribalization of politics and of society at large.

So why is this happening? And why is it happening now? There are at least three overlapping trends at work: the way in which *status* has replaced *survival* as our dominant societal imperative; the economic stagnation that has made politics into a series of zero-sum games; and finally, the *Black Mirror* world of networked communications that serves as a megaphone and a catalyst for both of these trends. In a nutshell, politics is eating the world, and it's making collective action and even the exercise of reason itself nearly impossible in what amounts to a culture-wide return to barbarism.

* * *

IN HIS BOOK *Unpopular Essays*, Bertrand Russell divides the misfortunes that can befall humanity into two general categories—those inflicted by nature, and those inflicted by other humans. As he points out, for most of human existence a good chunk of our suffering was caused by nature—things like famines and disease and the elements. But as civilization evolved, as we got smarter and richer and more organized, harms caused by other people increased, while those due to natural causes decreased. There's now less famine but more war. More generally, the growth of civilization shifted our concerns from *struggles against the elements* to *trying to deal with other people.* Our politics thus went from being focused on survival, to being obsessed with status.

This distinction between survival and status has deep philosophical roots. It goes back at least to Rousseau, who in his in his treatise *Emile, or On Education* make a distinction between what he calls *amour de soi* and *amour propre.* Both terms translate into English as "self-love," and each reflects a form of pride or self-respect. Rousseau sees *amour de soi*, which arises out of the need for survival or self- preservation that drives all animals, not just humans, as the more basic or primitive form of love. The self-respect that defines *amour de soi* has to do with one's personal wellbeing; it's the happy state that arises when you triumph over the elements by providing yourself and your loved ones with food and shelter and security in the struggle for survival.

In contrast, *amour propre* is the self-respect or pride that comes from comparing yourself with other people. It is a type of ego, or vanity, and is fundamentally about triumphing in any number of zero-sum status competitions. What feeds your *amour propre* is not, for example, building a house that keeps you and your family safe and warm or tending a garden or a farm that keeps you fed. It's about having a bigger house than your neighbour, a fancier car, a nicer lawn, a bigger barbecue, or going on more expensive or exotic vacations. We moderns regularly and unthinkingly engage in an enormous list of status competitions, to the point where we often don't realize just how much of our time is spent in a status struggle with other people.

Of course, even the state of nature that Rousseau described isn't completely free of *amour propre*—both forms of Rousseauian self-love exist in all human societies, however primitive or small-scale. The status-seeking at the heart of *amour propre* is simply what we call "politics" in the most general sense, as when we talk about "office politics." It even exists in non-human societies. Anyone who's read Frans de Waal's classic *Chimpanzee Politics*, about political rivalry and coalition-building within a troop of chimpanzees, can't help but be struck by how much the primates' gamesmanship and overlapping struggles for sex, power, and influence resemble what goes on in human affairs.

The course of the industrial age has witnessed the shift identified by Bertrand Russell: we've become so comfortable as a society that, for the vast majority of people in the West, mere survival has completely faded away as a concern. Instead, we spend more and more of our time and energy engaged in status competitions with other people. Our behaviours and beliefs no longer affect our survival in any serious way, they only impact our relative social, political, or economic status.

This has two important consequences. The first is that the need for our beliefs to connect or respond to reality has become increasingly unimportant. We are free to believe literally anything, from the wildest alt-right

QAnon political conspiracies to the wackiest Gwyneth Paltrow health-nut fantasies of the contemporary wellness movement. None of it really matters—the lights still come on in your house, your car still runs, the grocery stores remain stocked with food. As J Storrs Hall puts it, humans have an enormous capacity to believe things not because they are true, but because they are advantageous to hold. Once upon a time, it was more advantageous to know the facts of the world than not to, so we developed science. Today, our beliefs are less a reflection of our reality than a means of identifying our respective political tribes and negotiating our status within them.

The upshot is that belief has an increasingly Veblenian character.[36] As Hall puts it, "The result of this is that we have major social institutions whose support comes in substantial part from virtue signalling rather than from actual useful results... they include health care, education, and environmental and safety regulation, among others."[37] "Luxury beliefs"—such as the denial of climate change by the right, or the persistent denial of personal responsibility by the left—do harm people, eventually. But they tend not to impact the people at the top of the status ladder; it's those lower in the hierarchy who'll ultimately suffer.

The second consequence of belief becoming a form of status competition is that life increasingly takes on the character of a zero-sum game, where one person's gain is another's loss. This is an inherent feature of status competitions, and it has a number of predictable effects, including making people more distrustful and resentful, while making it hard for them to commit to the limits on their freedoms that make positive-sum collective action possible. And all of this becomes further amplified during extended periods of economic stagnation, where the absence of significant growth only increases the status stakes.

* * *

ONE OF THE more pervasive luxury beliefs of our time is the one—often packaged with neo-Malthusian warnings about the dangers of overpopulation and the planet's finite resources—that says economic growth doesn't matter; or, worse, that it's actually a bad thing. In recent years there has even been a turn toward the idea that growth is antithetical to human flourishing or happiness.[38] But as John Kenneth Galbraith once noted, "Wealth is not without its advantages and the case to the contrary, although it has often been made, has never proved widely persuasive."

There are good reasons why this is the case. As the economy grows, we get richer and more productive and experience a rise in our standard of living. Just about everyone today has access to electricity, central heating, refrigeration, and indoor plumbing. The penetration rate of consumer items like flat-screen televisions, mobile phones, broadband internet, and gaming consoles is very high, even within the lower-middle class. Aside from the homeless, the poor in our society do not suffer from the deprivations and miseries that were the norm for even the well-to-do a hundred years ago. Almost everyone today lives in a heated home with running hot and cold water, has access to vaccines and antibiotics and pain killers, and enjoys radio, television, and other entertainments.

In the United States, the internet penetration level is 90 percent of the population. Economic growth has made our lives longer and more comfortable, giving us a higher standard of living and more leisure time than our grandparents could only have dreamed of.

These facts are widely accepted. But it is also widely understood that economic growth comes at a cost. Part of that cost is environmental—the depletion of natural resources, pollution, and climate change being three of the most obvious downsides. But we also worry about growth's other effects, such as increasing economic and social inequality, or the spiritual price we pay for living in an alienating and shallow consumer society. As a result, we find ourselves unhappy with, or just embarrassed by, our ever-rising standard of living, to the point where many people see further economic growth as unnecessary or even morally objectionable.

There is no question that growth's material benefits are subject to diminishing returns. There is a sizable literature exploring the idea that the welfare benefits of growth—that is, gains in the standard living, life expectancy, and even happiness—arrive pretty early on in the process. Additional growth doesn't make us any healthier, it also doesn't make us any happier. Beyond around US$12k in per capita GDP, most of the "extra" growth tends to get funnelled into an ever-lengthening string of arms races and zero-sum status competitions for things such as fancier cars, more exotic vacations, or more exclusive private schools.[39] This inclines many people to the obvious conclusion that we should stop trying to grow the economy and focus, instead, on more inclusive measures of well-being, such "Gross National Happiness."

And when it comes to the Great Stagnation—whatever its causes—many people are similarly inclined to just shrug and wonder what the big deal is.

But there's another way of looking at growth that doesn't depend on singing the virtues of its material outcomes. Economic growth doesn't just make us better off, it also makes us, collectively, better people by making us more tolerant and accepting of diversity. It also enhances social mobility, gives us a greater sense of fairness and equality, and increases our commitment to democratic ideals and institutions.

The key point here is that it's *the growth itself* that matters, not how it affects our absolute living standards. It's the simple fact of economic expansion that inclines people towards feelings of openness and toleration and that inspires trust in our democratic institutions. Just as the knowledge the pie will keep getting bigger makes people more generous in the divvying up of that pie, the sense that we can expect things to get even better—no matter where we currently are on the development curve—acts as a sort of bellows of fellow-feeling, making people more hopeful for the future and more generous-minded. More than anything else, the mere fact of growth is a signal that the future will be better than the past.

Unsurprisingly, the opposite holds during periods of stagnation, when zero-sum thinking kicks in. When the economy stops growing or even starts to shrink, people become fearful for the future, suspicious of immigrants and diversity in general, and distrustful of democracy. Stagnation breeds authoritarianism—that, of course, is one of the great lessons of the 1930s, as the Great Depression drove diverse, democratic populations toward nationalism and into the arms of fascist dictators. While there are no iron-clad laws of history, economic stagnation and the decline of liberal democracy are strongly linked.[40]

Nowhere is this more clear than in the recent history of the United States. As the Harvard economist Benjamin Friedman put it in his book *The Moral Consequences of Economic Growth*, "The consequence of the stagnation that lasted from the mid-1970s until the mid-1990s was, in numerous dimensions, a fraying of the U.S. social fabric. It was no coincidence that during this period popular antipathy to immigrants resurfaced to an extent not known in the United States since before World War II." Remarkably, Friedman's book came out in 2006, when it was still an open question whether the return to the higher levels of growth of the late 1990s would prove sustainable. The answer came two years later, when the financial crisis of 2008 catalyzed the Great Recession by cratering the finances of the middle class and those struggling to join it.

The result of these two trendlines—the dominance of luxury-belief-driven status competition in a period of extended economic stagnation—was a brew of identity politics, political tribalism, and cultural warfare that would have been bad enough on its own. It's when you toss it all into the seething cauldron of social media that things start to get really toxic.

* * *

SOME HAVE JOKED that the plot of every episode of the popular dystopian sci-fi TV show *Black Mirror* could be summarized as "what if phones, but too much?"[41]

This little meme perfectly captures one of the show's recurring themes: namely, that our fraught relationship with technology boils down to fears about the baleful influence of mobile networked communication. The joke also winks broadly at the fact that everyone is fully aware of what's going on. Smartphone use, in other words, has become such a massive social problem that making wry jokes about it is all we can really do.

We're talking about social media, the broad constellation of websites, apps, and platforms that includes video sites like YouTube and TikTok, photo-based social networks such as Instagram, messaging apps like WhatsApp or Slack, and the more general sharing sites like Twitter and Facebook. We can view social media as a mixed blessing and conclude that, as with all technological developments, from fire to the wheel to the telegraph, something is obviously gained, but something valuable is lost along the way. Unlike with previous innovations, what's become clear about social media over the past half decade though, is that a lot more has been lost than gained.

What's notable about social media is that its most vicious critics are often its users. If you spend any time at all on Facebook or Twitter you'll quickly see that pretty much everyone agrees how awful it is. One of Twitter users' most common descriptors for the platform is "this hellsite." Though the case against social media is well known, it is worth revisiting for the way it sums up our civilization decline.

The first thing worth keeping in mind about the various social media is just how different they are from virtually every form of media that came before them.

Their most relevant features are that they are instant, public, global, anonymous, and persistent.

Looking back at the world before Twitter or Facebook or TikTok, it feels like everything was happening in slow motion, like the way mail used to be delivered by ship or how messages used to be relayed by pony. A newspaper op-ed would garner a response a few days after being written, and a few letters to the editor would then trickle in for publication maybe on the following weekend. Now, the conversation happens more or less in real time as the distinction between comment and response, action and reaction, has collapsed.

Social media are also intrinsically public, which of course the media has always been. But what's different now is that posts to social media are, pretty much by definition, designed to be shared as widely as possible. Conversations used to be restricted by the scope or reach of the media in which they appeared—local in the case of a metropolitan newspaper, radio show, or television broadcast; national in the case of select newspapers and television networks. Now all media is global, for all intents and purposes.

The instant, public, and global nature of social media would alone be enough to make them qualitatively different from anything that came before. But two other features of social media serve to amplify their effect and, in many cases, their toxicity.

One is the fact that many social media platforms allow for, or even encourage, anonymity or pseudonymity. It's not news that people behave differently under the cloak of anonymity than how they do when they know they're being watched or can be identified. In *The Republic*, Plato invokes the myth of the Ring of Gyges, a magical artifact that renders the wearer invisible, to ask whether someone would continue to act justly if they didn't have to worry about getting caught behaving in an unjust manner. Thanks to Twitter egg accounts, we now have the definitive answer to that question.

Two other aspects of social media whose effects are only now becoming obvious are its persistence and searchability. Even the most offhand joke or snide remark posted years or decades ago can be quickly dug up and shared as if it appeared just minutes previously. This has its amusements. For every outrageous action or outright hypocrisy Donald Trump committed during his presidency, for instance, a tweet could always be found from years gone by showing him holding the exact opposite position. But more often than not, social media's permanence has been marshalled in the service of cancel culture, to take short remarks from long ago out of context, or hold young adults unreasonably accountable for the idle thoughts of their adolescence.

Perhaps no one put it as pithily as the writer Becca Rothfeld, who tweeted during the summer of 2020 (on a Twitter account that she has since, tellingly, deleted): "I think it is frankly ~insane~ to deny the psychological, social, and political significance of the fact that, for the first time in human history, you can be publicly shamed on a global scale by hundreds of thousands of online strangers."[42]

Finally, it cannot be overstated just how addictive social media are. They are designed from the ground up to trigger the quick-response elements of our psychology, with the rush of endorphins that comes with every like,

share, favourite, retweet, or comment. This addictive-
ness is tightly related to the role social media play in our
quest for status. That itself is nothing new—status-seeking is the oldest human instinct, after all. What is new is
how the vectors for status-seeking are now piped directly
into peoples' phones instead of being mediated through
things like consumer goods (nicest car, coolest concert
t-shirt, etc).

The upshot of all of this is that status-seeking via
social media, especially on open and anonymous platforms such as Twitter, has put political polarization on
steroids. One of the best ways of communicating an "I'm
better than you" message is through virtue-signalling: an
expression or statement intended to promote one's own
righteousness or moral superiority. The competitive
indignation that results from this feeds both the hostile
anti-elitism of the alt-right, and the crushing identity
politics of the ctrl-left. On the left, the standard require-
ment that everyone pay lip service to identity politics has
resulted in nonstop online morality policing. On the
right, traditional animosity toward the "cultural elite"
has turned into an unhinged rejection of fact and argument, authority and expertise—the result being
widespread misogyny, anti-Semitism, and the proliferation of partisan propaganda that we politely call "fake
news." In both cases, the pressure to conform to the most
extreme position is huge.[43]

It's important to appreciate the strategic position this
puts everyone in. Engaging with social media amounts
to joining a global, real-time, prisoner's dilemma with
Hunger Games-level stakes. It's a massive collective action
problem, where almost everyone ends up taking a posi-

tion they wouldn't otherwise hold, condoning behaviours they wouldn't otherwise support, simply because of the built-in logic of the platform environment. Like every collective action problem, this one can't be solved through the patient application of individual reason. You can't reason your way out of social media's toxicity any more than you can reason your way out of a traffic jam or an arms race.

But it's actually even worse than that. The problem we now face isn't that reason is ineffective when confronted with the logic of digital culture. It's that digital culture works against reason itself, making it increasingly hard for us to behave rationally even when we most desperately want to.

4. On Reason

ON JANUARY 23, 2020, the Bulletin of the Atomic Scientists, a nonprofit organization devoted to global science and security issues, moved the hands of its Doomsday Clock to 100 seconds to midnight. As the accompanying press release noted, this put humanity "closer than ever" to catastrophe. Given that the clock has kept watch over our drive for self-destruction through the Suez Crisis, the Cuban Missile Crisis, the Reagan administration's nuclear sabre-rattling, and the terrorist attacks of September 11, 2001, one wonders what happened in early 2020 to merit such a fearful move, especially since the decision to change the Clock's time was made before the pandemic had been declared.

To understand this, it helps to understand the evolution of the Doomsday Clock itself, which was conceived in 1947 by some of the scientists who worked on the Manhattan Project to raise public awareness about the threat of nuclear weapons. As the Bulletin puts it, the clock uses "the imagery of apocalypse (midnight) and the contemporary idiom of nuclear explosion (countdown to zero) to convey threats to humanity and the planet." The decision to move or leave the minute hand of the Clock in place is made each year by the Bulletin's various trustees, based on their evaluation of the world's current vulnerability to catastrophe.

So while the Doomsday Clock was originally conceived as a measure of our proximity to nuclear war, it has evolved into a generalized warning against war, climate change, and various technological threats. In moving the minute hand to 100 seconds to midnight, the Bulletin was signalling both ongoing threats of global security and the reality of climate change, but also the growing problem of disinformation and the poisoning of the media ecosystem.[44]

This shift in emphasis is understandable. What we consider the biggest threats facing humanity have always been a moving target. For most of the twentieth century, the number one fear was all-out nuclear Armageddon. That faded after the fall of the Berlin wall, and for a while after 9/11 it looked like Islamic terrorism might pose an existential threat—if not to humanity, then at least to the West. But terrorism, too, has become part of modernity's background radiation. Meanwhile, anthropogenic climate change, aka global warming, has emerged as the most urgent and compelling concern for the human race even as rational debate around the subject has been confounded by the proliferation of fake news.

In the briefing that accompanied the announcement of the moving of the hands of the Doomsday Clock, the Bulletin made a number of straightforward policy recommendations. The US and Russia should re-engage with arms-reduction talks. World leaders should re-commit themselves to the carbon-reduction targets of the Paris Climate Agreement. The international community must establish norms to discourage the misuse of science, while citizens must insist on facts, discount nonsense, and demand action from their governments. In short, global collective action, underwritten by the clear exercise of reason, must prevail.

Unfortunately, it's becoming apparent that reason can't help us, since it is reason's very workings that are part of the problem.

* * *

WE STARTED TO figure out just how defective our reasoning apparatus is forty or fifty years ago, thanks to some groundbreaking experiments in social psychology. Probably the most influential was the work of the Israeli researchers Daniel Kahneman and Amos Tversky, whose "prospect theory" explored the shortcuts, rules of thumb, and blind spots of our minds; the heuristics and biases that infect all the judgments and decision-making that go on inside our skulls. Their work spawned an enormous academic literature that, a few decades later, was taken up by popular writers including Malcolm Gladwell, Dan Ariely, David Brooks, and Daniel Gilbert... the list goes on, and gets longer with every book season. (Perhaps out of a desire to finally cash in on his own work, Daniel Kahneman produced an excellent primer on his research in 2011 called *Thinking, Fast and Slow*.)

What emerged from this research is what's sometimes referred to as "dual process theory," which posits that we are cognitively equipped with two distinct modes or systems of reasoning. System 1 is fast, automatic, and opaque, and represents what we usually call our "gut instinct." Evolutionarily speaking, it is ancient, and well-adapted for survival in small groups of hominids. System 1 is activated when we react in fear to a big hairy spider, or in disgust to the sight of worms. We rely on System 1 when we catch a ball thrown from a few feet away, or when we're driving straight on a highway on a clear day. These things take little to no conscious effort—indeed, it takes effort to *not* do them.

Overlaid on this massively parallel System 1 structure is the slow, serial, and explicit System 2, which is what we generally mean when we talk about "reason." Where System 1 relies on associative reasoning and emotional resonances in order to offer rough-and-ready judgments, System 2 allows us to entertain hypotheticals and engage in abstract, precise reasoning. We need System 2 when we're first learning to play a musical instrument, trying to find a parking spot on a busy street, or when we're asked to multiply two three-digit numbers. System 2 is also what allows us to escape our tribal instincts and recognize when large-scale cooperation is in our long-term and collective interest. If System 1 represents our barbaric past, System 2 is the hope of civilization.

We actually need both systems, and each serves us well in its proper domain. The problem is, the original "proper domain" for System 1 was the African savannah, where its biases and snap judgments were reliably correlated with predictable features of the environment. The various dispositions and biases that are baked into our cognitive architecture, and which enable us to make snap decisions in hostile environments where survival is an ongoing struggle, are increasingly maladapted in the modern world where our challenges go beyond mere survival.

As a result, our relationship with reason is a swiss-cheese of paradox. One way of noting the paradox is this: all the expertise, brainpower, evidence, and logic we bring to bear on a problem offers no guarantee that we'll get anywhere close to the truth. It turns out that we're extremely good at deploying logic, gathering evidence, and making arguments to justify our pre-existing instincts and intuitions, which means it's just as likely as not that the instruments of reason will become tools for rational-ization, self-deception, and special pleading. This is actually a lot more worrisome than it might initially appear, because it means that it isn't enough for us to ignore those who argue in bad faith or who act out of transparently cynical motives. Even if we believe every-one is arguing in good faith and is trying to do what's best by their own lights, it's hard to accept that those lights obscure a lot more than they illuminate.

At the heart of this lies what might be the most trou-bling paradox of all; namely, that it's often in our private interest to endorse beliefs that have no basis in either reason or the senses. Borrowing an idea from the legal scholar Dan Kahan, Steven Pinker argues that we are trapped in a society-wide collective action problem, which he calls "the tragedy of the belief commons." Like all collective action problems, this one posits a scenario where behaviour that is rational for each individual becomes collectively self-defeating—think of what hap-pens when a crowd rushes toward the exits during a fire alarm, or when everyone repeatedly changes lanes in heavy traffic.

The tragedy of the belief commons (which Kahan calls "the tragedy of the risk-perception commons")[45] arises because there are times when it is rational for each of us as individuals to hold certain beliefs not because of how the world is, but because of who we are or want to be. We're not just a social species, we're a tribal one as well, with our group identities giving purpose and meaning to our lives. But being a member of a group usually involves believing certain things that are particular to that group, and if that belief boils down to a contest between reality and our sense of self, or the esteem of our peers, well, so much the worse for reality. We're all familiar with this sort of "expressive rationality"—raise your hand if you ever pretended to like a band because the cool kids all did—but it becomes perverse when the price of admission to a given club or tribe is the embrace of unfounded ideas or outright nonsense.

Just as organized crime families require new recruits to commit atrocities in order to prove their commitment, preposterous beliefs are more effective signals of loyalty to a coalition than are reasonable ones. Anyone can claim that rocks fall down rather than up, but only a person who is truly committed to the cause has reason to say that God is three persons but also one person, or that the Democratic Party ran a child sex ring out of a Washington pizzeria.

Kahan saw the paradox arising in the context of evidence for climate change. He and his colleagues tested the thesis that the main reason there is still controversy over climate change is because of a lack of popular knowledge of the relevant science. But what they found was surprising: greater scientific knowledge simply led to greater cultural polarization, where people who were predisposed to dismiss evidence for climate change became even more dismissive, while those who were predisposed to believe the evidence for climate change became more convinced as their knowledge increased.

The unfortunate consequence of the tragedy of the belief commons is that what's rational for individuals to believe, given their desire to have certain identities, a) isn't always based on pure reason, and b) isn't always good for society as a whole. This amounts to something along the lines of: Humans are relentlessly driven to organize themselves into tribes, us versus them, in-group/out-group. So much so that we have trouble seeing how much all this tribalism works against our common interest. This is why telling people they need to just "think harder," or use more reason, isn't going to work any more than telling someone that driving sensibly will get them out of a traffic jam quicker. It isn't just that self-interest sometimes drives us to bypass reason, it's that our current social environment is set up to actively discourage it.

* * *

EVER BEEN IN a casino? They're nothing like what we see in the movies. There are no high, vaulted ceilings and bright chandeliers. There's no piano tinkling gently in the background while dashing men in tuxedos throw dice as gorgeous women in gowns lean over their shoulder sipping a cocktail. In a real casino, the ceilings are low, the lighting is dark, and there are no windows, clocks, or other means of distinguishing night from day, dusk from dawn. The gambling infrastructure is the decor, it's loud and overwhelming, like a carnival midway built into the sides of a rabbit warren. The first thing you see when you arrive are slot machines, and they're the last thing you see when you leave. Slot machines are the functional equivalent of the pleasure levers rats are induced to push in addiction research.

A casino, then, is a big engine designed to do one thing: separate you from your money in the most efficient way possible. It does this using every trick we've learned to take advantage of our deficient rational faculties. Experienced casino-goers know this, so they take steps to mitigate the damage before they even enter the casino. They don't accept the free drinks, they bring only as much money as they're willing to lose, and they quit while they're ahead. It's difficult and exhausting, but it can be done. The problem is that the whole world—our entire built environment—is starting to take on the character of a giant casino.

Do you ever get the feeling that at every moment, someone, some institution or business, or some algorithm, is doing its best to disable your rational faculties in order to trick System 1 into handing over your attention, your identity, or your money? Well, take a look around. The "exit through the gift shop" logic of the art gallery or museum has become a bit of a cliché; less well known is the way supermarkets are designed to mimic certain aspects of a casino—especially the layout that carefully channels you through sections where the owners want you to spend the most time. The gum and chocolate bars at the checkout are the grocery equivalent of slot machines. Stores like Costco go one further, deliberately refusing to put signs in the aisles in order to force customers to wander around shopping more or less at random. Then there's Ikea, where the confusing, maze-like layout could have been cribbed straight from a casino design manual.

But however bad the real world is, things are even worse online, where casino design principles are built into the very foundations of how we acquire and organize information, how we process the world around us, and how we conduct our politics. Go on over to Amazon, which works on the same trick-driven principles, but with algorithms shaping your path through the maze in real time. Entertainment? Netflix, with its random, algorithm-created categories like "Animal Cartoons Promoting Friendship" or "Period Pieces About Royalty Based on Real Life" turns the process of choosing something to watch into another version of playing the slots. Mobile gaming is a casino, as is, increasingly, the console market. Fox News is a casino, as is most cable news programming. Google search, Facebook news, Tinder and Bumble, Twitter and Instagram? They're all casinos, designed to disrupt our ability to engage in focused, System 2-type thinking.

Here's what's happening: Our entire cultural infrastructure is steadily evolving to take advantage of the weaknesses in our brains. Specifically, it is evolving to take advantage of the bottlenecks of System 2-type reasoning and to exploit the biases and shortcuts evolution has hardwired into System 1. Our attention is valuable, not just to capitalists, but to marketers, politicians, and propagandists of all sorts, and the techniques for grabbing our attention are undergoing a fierce evolutionary development. Reason is being elbowed off the playing field, with the result is that the gains of civilization, the proceeds of the Enlightenment, are at risk of being reversed.

We're rushing back into barbarism, and it isn't clear we have the wherewithal to stop it.[46]

Why does reason have so much trouble getting a purchase in the modern world? It helps to recognize how heavily human rationality is *scaffolded*. When we try to reason with our bare brains, it's hard to get anything serious done. Sure, doing 2+2 in your head is simple, but how about 172 x 423? Better get out a pencil and paper. Most of us have no problem accepting that we can't do basic multiplication in our heads, or that we need a calendar to keep track of our appointments, but we don't scale that acceptance to our most sophisticated institutions and enterprises. The truth is, the vast majority of "reasoning" that goes on in our society isn't done in peoples' heads, it's done by the scaffolding around us.

To give one example, think about the path a bill takes through parliament. There are eight distinct stages, from its notice and placement on the Order Paper, three readings in the House of Commons, consideration by committee and by the Senate, and, finally, Royal Assent—the process can take months or even years. But the glacial pace of legislation is a feature, not a bug: parliament is a machine for activating System 2 reasoning. By slowing everything down, it allows plenty of room for the exercise of reason and deliberation.

This is the core insight of the conservative critique of the original Enlightenment. Our civilization is built into our environment, our practices and institutions and technologies, and we are in the process of changing that environment in ways that undermine System 2 and serve System 1's casino-like impulses.

The result is that even as we get more access to expertise and information than ever before, we find it harder to behave rationally because our environment is becoming increasingly hostile to reason by constantly changing and adding to our collective cognitive load. We're running to stand still, which has led to all these paradoxes of reason. Ultimately, behaving more rationally, or committing to Enlightenment virtues, aren't things we can do on our own. And that's because reason isn't something we have, it's something we do. It's an achievement, not an endowment. And that achievement is necessarily collective, environmental, and institutional.

To truly reclaim the virtues of the Enlightenment we would have to take a common decision to have a culture of a certain sort, to take collective action to reinforce the institutions of rationality that have served us so well for so long, but which are now threatened. It would have to be the sort of collective action that free societies typically only take when faced with an existential threat from without. But the barbarians aren't at the gates. They're in our heads. Our System 1 dispositions are the barbarians we've spent centuries fighting off, and now we're using whatever reserves of reason we have at our disposal to set them free.

There's no obvious way for the genie to get back in the bottle. As we are slowly coming to realize, our powers of reasoning are highly maladaptive, to the degree that they're ultimately going to serve as agents of our civilizational decline. All of these problems collided during the COVID-19 pandemic, which saw an immense gap open up across the West between the success of our scientific response on the one hand, and the systematic failure of our political response on the other.

5. On the Pandemic

ONE OF THE more startling aspects of the early weeks of the COVID-19 pandemic was how fast everything happened, on a number of fronts. It was New Year's Eve 2019 when Chinese authorities first confirmed they were treating dozens of cases of a pneumonia of "unknown cause." The first deaths from this pneumonia were reported via Chinese state media on January 11. The first cases outside mainland China were reported on January 20, and the first reported case in the United States was on the 21st. Two days later, the centre of the outbreak in China, the city of Wuhan in Hubei Province, was completely sealed off from the rest of the country; construction was begun on an emergency hospital, which opened ten days later.

On January 30, the WHO declared a global health emergency as the virus continued to spread. Over the next few weeks, there were outbreaks across Asia, Europe, North America, and the Middle East. Several serious outbreaks on cruise ships hit the industry hard. Even as the Chinese seemed to get things under control, South Korea, Iran, and Italy became regional hotspots. Governments scrambled to respond, but on March 11, the WHO bowed to reality and declared a global pandemic.

When the histories are written about the global response to the novel coronavirus, two things will stand out. The first is the enormous divergence between what science was able to achieve in a very short time, and the capacity and willingness of governments and public health authorities to make use of those achievements. The second is the stark divergence in the speed and effectiveness of various government responses, in particular between governments in Asia and Oceania (which were largely effective) and governments in Europe and North America (which, for the most part, were not).

Taken together, these two strands help illustrate some of the central theses being advanced in this book about our society's state of decline. These include political lethargy and lassitude in the face of a once-in-a-century public health crisis; a failure of strategic preparedness and lack of state capacity combined with regulatory inflexibility; and a tribalistic political culture increasingly detached from reality and hostile to collective action.

* * *

WHEN THE NOVEL coronavirus that became known as COVID-19 exploded into a global pandemic in March 2020, prospects for a quick solution in the form of an effective treatment, or even a vaccine, were pretty grim. Part of the problem was an initial misdiagnosis of the virus as an exceptionally vicious respiratory ailment. As a result, initial treatment strategies often involved the assumption that many patients would need to be on ventilators. Sourcing an adequate ventilator supply, along with the drugs that need to be given to intubated patients, thus became a pressing early problem.

Scientists eventually figured out that COVID wasn't a pulmonary disease but rather a cardiovascular disease, where the virus targeted the endothelium, the layer of cells lining the inside of every blood vessel. This discovery helped explain many of the stranger symptoms of COVID-19 infection, including blood clots, strange rashes, myocarditis, and a spike in cases of Kawasaki disease among children. It also helped them zero in on more effective drug treatments.

As for the hopes for a vaccine, while there were already a number of vaccines available that gave dogs protection against coronavirus infections, no coronavirus vaccine had ever successfully been developed for use in humans. There are a number of reasons why that's the case, including the fact that the upper respiratory tract is a difficult area for a vaccine to target.

Even successful vaccines usually take years to develop. A typical timeline, which includes vaccine design, pre-clinical trials, phase 1-3 clinical trials, and then the regulatory approval process, is anywhere from five to ten years. In the spring of 2020, as the first wave of the pandemic was building across the globe, more than seventy vaccine development efforts were underway worldwide. Yet by early summer 2020 experts were still cautioning that the absolute best-case scenario for an accelerated COVID-19 vaccine was eighteen months, which would mean delivery somewhere around the end of 2021.

At the time, few people were aware that an effective vaccine had already been developed. On Friday, January 10, 2020, Chinese health officials posted the genetic sequence of the novel coronavirus to the internet. Two researchers from Moderna, a Massachusetts-based pharmaceutical startup that had never produced a vaccine before, downloaded the sequence, and within a day had designed the proteins for a vaccine. They gave the design to Moderna on January 13, and six weeks later the company was shipping doses to be used in clinical trials.[47] On December 18, the FDA gave emergency-use approval for the Moderna vaccine, which is itself remarkable. More remarkable still is that it was actually the second vaccine given such approval. A week earlier, the FDA had approved a vaccine developed jointly by Pfizer/BioNTech, with the first shots going into arms on December 14, 2020.

At the heart of this effort was a program called Operation Warp Speed, initiated by the US government to invest in the rapid research and development of COVID-19 vaccines and therapies. The US$10 billion program provided funding to pharmaceutical companies to invest in manufacturing supply chains even before their vaccines had been proven effective, let alone approved for use. In return, the US government was able to secure early delivery of hundreds of millions of doses for American citizens. By the end of February 2020, three of the companies that OWS invested in had brought successful COVID-19 vaccines to market, including Moderna, Oxford-AstraZeneca, and Johnson & Johnson.

Operation Warp Speed takes its name from the fictional warp drive that allows for faster-than-light travel within the Star Trek universe. But it also contains echoes of the phrase that John F Kennedy used when he was exhorting Congress to fund the lunar mission. There was a time when speed, freedom, and democracy were virtual synonyms, or at least just different ways of describing the same underlying faith in our collective ability to drive progress. Kennedy's phrase about "the full speed of freedom" was intended as a slogan of optimism about the future.

Despite the success of Operation Warp Speed, it's hard not to see it as something that succeeded despite our abilities, not because of them. It is less a harbinger of our technocratic future than a reminder of the extent to which that future has simply failed to materialize. More than anything, the big lesson of the COVID-19 pandemic will be just how poorly the democracies of the West managed the most significant global crisis in almost a century.

* * *

THE TEXTBOOK PUBLIC health response to a viral outbreak goes like this: First, you lock down society as much as possible to "flatten the curve" of transmission and get the cases under control. Then you keep pressing down on the curve until the contagion's basic reproduction number (the Ro or "R-nought") gets to the point where recovery rates outpace hospitalizations, so hospitals and other health services aren't overwhelmed.

Once this is done, society can slowly start to reopen— not all at once, mind you, but in a managed or staged return, because any loosening of the lockdown risks re-starting the outbreak. To avoid a "pumping the brakes" scenario, where you ping-pong between opening and full lockdown, it's important to do what's called "test, trace, and isolate": Significantly increase the rate of testing of the population; trace back to the recent contacts of anyone who tests positive, and isolate them to snuff out any chains of transmission before they become uncontrollable. You keep this up until, hopefully, the virus burns itself out, you find some effective treatments, or you develop a vaccine.

The test, trace, and isolate response works best when there are relatively few cases and contacts to trace. Once you get "community transmission" (that is, a situation where you and the authorities have no idea where you caught the virus), controlling an outbreak becomes much more difficult.

In the pandemic's early days, South Korea set the gold standard for the execution of this strategy. In the aftermath of the 2015 MERS outbreak that killed 186 people in that country, the South Korean government passed an infectious disease control act prioritizing openness and transparency at the expense of privacy and individual freedom. The act stipulates that as long as patients aren't publicly identified, authorities can publish information about their movements, contacts, and activities. When it came to dealing with the COVID-19 outbreak that hit the country early and hard, South Korea was ruthless about using digital technologies to track possible contacts. Health authorities were given access to CCTV footage, cellphone GPS data, credit card information, and other records, with updates and information sent directly to every smartphone in the country.[48]

The South Korean effort was the perfect technocratic alliance of science, technology, and public health bureaucracy. And it was extremely successful. A year into the pandemic, Korea had recorded around 80,000 cases and fewer than 1,500 deaths, one of the lowest per capita death rates in the developed world. There was every reason to believe that countries in the West would be able to replicate this success. Test, trace, and isolate quickly formed the basis of virtually every coronavirus containment plan in Europe and North America, with the only other option being the "herd immunity" theory that the UK started but quickly abandoned, and which was not widely attempted outside of Sweden. The results of these experiments might be charitably described as mixed.[49]

But like any plan with a lot of moving parts, test/trace/isolate (TTI) needs to succeed at every stage for it to work at all. For many countries, including the UK, Canada, and the United States, the first major bottleneck was testing, which proved difficult to achieve at the necessary scale. Early on, a big part of the problem was a worldwide shortage of the nasopharyngeal swabs used for collecting samples from the back of the patient's nasal passage. There was also a widespread shortage of the PCR reagents for the machines that do the testing, and a dearth of trained professionals to execute the actual tests. (In Canada, emergency proposals to cut corners on regulations and press graduate students into service doing the tests was strongly resisted by the national lab technician certification body).

But even once most countries had managed to ramp up testing to acceptable levels (something that took months to accomplish), other obstacles quickly appeared. In Canada, outside of the provinces that had managed to keep caseloads extremely low (such as British Columbia and the Atlantic provinces), contact tracing proved extremely challenging. Authorities had trouble finding enough people to do the tracing, and it didn't help that the federal government was essentially paying people, including university students, to sit at home and do nothing all summer long. But Canadians also proved highly reluctant to accept the levels of surveillance and intrusions into privacy that proper contact tracing would require.

In sharp contrast with the South Korean government's ruthless efforts, the federal government in Ottawa was so leery of looking intrusive that it was reluctant to even acknowledge that it was considering making use of tracking software. Meanwhile, various provinces went their own way in developing contact tracing apps. When Ottawa finally released a version of the app developed by Apple and Microsoft, it was so stripped down in deference to privacy concerns that it turned out to be basically useless.

Compounding the tracing issue were failures of intergovernmental coordination. In order for the tracing app to be effective, users who tested positive needed to get a code from the provincial authority that would then be entered into the app in order to alert possible contacts. But a year into the pandemic, fewer than 5 percent of all those who tested positive in Canada for COVID-19 were being given the code, and of those, only four fifths bothered to enter it. In the end, test, trace, and isolate never got off the ground in Canada: the app had virtually no impact on slowing or limiting the spread of the virus.[50] The provincial governments that were most affected by the virus (namely, Quebec and Ontario) never came close to developing an adequate testing regime, and the public never acquired what one British health official described as the necessary "Dunkirk mentality" for effective contact tracing.

While some of these missteps and miscalculations could be chalked up to the fog-of-war chaos of the pandemic's early weeks, many actually predated the appearance of COVID-19 on our shores. For example, in the aftermath of the SARS epidemic that killed forty-three people in Ontario in 2003, federal and provincial officials were lambasted for their lack of emergency preparedness and poor response. Yet when the COVID-19 pandemic arrived, it was almost like nothing had been learned.

To give just two examples: At the provincial level, in the early rush to source adequate amounts of personal protective equipment (PPE) for medical staff, it was revealed that Ontario had allowed its post-SARS emergency stockpile of 55 million N95 masks to expire without replacing it. Meanwhile, in Ottawa, it turned out that the federal government had largely dismantled Canada's Global Public Health Intelligence Network (GPHIN), the early warning system for infectious disease that was providing the World Health Organization with as much as 20 percent of its open-source intelligence.[51] As part of a plan to put the network's resources to domestic use, many of the staff had been parcelled out to other functions in the public service, in particular to Heath Canada's vaping policy desk.

Examples like these were far from isolated mistakes or bureaucratic one-offs. This fundamental failure of the technocratic, strategic, command-and-control state was replicated across Canada's pandemic response, at virtually every level of government and across a whole swath of responsible ministries and agencies. Whether it was maintaining acceptable stockpiles of PPE, securing the nation's borders, implementing a robust testing regimen, properly tracing contacts, overseeing and enforcing quarantine or self-isolation orders, guaranteeing safe work conditions for temporary foreign workers, managing and staffing long-term care facilities—if a ball were being tossed, it's safe to say that some Canadian government or regulatory agency was dropping it.[52]

Meanwhile, the officials who were the public face of the pandemic response found themselves wrong-footed from the very start. Not only were Canadian health officials reluctant to acknowledge the threat from COVID-19, their response was variously sluggish, uncertain, politicized, and condescending. Whether it was the effectiveness of travel bans, the usefulness of masks, or the merits of rapid testing—the last of which was never implemented in any significant way despite clear evidence of its effectiveness in situations of uncontrolled community spread—Canada's public health officials were repeatedly forced into complete reversals, quickly trying to implement policies they'd initially refused to even consider. This herky-jerky approach to policy-making and communications continued with the rollout of the vaccines well into 2021, with public faith in the safety of the Oxford-AstraZeneca undermined by poor risk management surrounding eligibility.

What's interesting, and concerning, is the extent to which, when it came to managing the pandemic, Canada was hardly an outlier amongst its so-called peer countries.

* * *

FROM THE VERY beginning, one of the more confounding things about the COVID-19 coronavirus was how variable and unpredictable its effects were. This is true of individual cases, but equally so when it comes to outcomes by country. To put it directly, some countries did much better than others in managing the pandemic. And while some of the correlations are what one might have predicted going into it, a lot of what happened is very surprising.

For example, you might have anticipated that countries led by right-wing populists would struggle with the pandemic. This was certainly borne out by the skyrocketing caseloads in countries like Brazil, the UK, and the United States. But would you have guessed that Sweden and Holland would have some of the highest infection rates in the world? Or that Belgium, followed by the Balkan countries, would have the highest per capita death rates in the world?

Teasing out the cause and effect here, figuring out which policies were effective and which were just theatre, will be part of a major post-pandemic international research project that will undertake years of detailed analysis. But some coarse-grained patterns have already emerged. One is that the Western democracies of Europe and North America generally did very poorly across the board, while countries in Asia and Oceania, including Australia and New Zealand, were very effective in controlling the spread of the virus.[53]

Journalistic shorthand often put Canada's and Europe's poor pandemic responses to an inability to "do logistics," or of a lack of "state capacity." In political science terms, state capacity refers to the ability of a state to marshal resources in the pursuit of certain goals, and to effectively implement policies and programs that achieve those goals. In Canada, the failure of civilian powers to effectively use state capacity to manage the pandemic was so striking that both Ontario's provincial government and the federal government in Ottawa hired retired army generals to oversee their vaccination programs. The feeling was that if there was one institution that could "do logistics" in the country, it was the military.

Saying that we're bad at logistics or lack state capacity gives the problem a name, but it doesn't really explain it. So what does? One possible answer is we're bad at logistics because we don't have to be good at it. The longer explanation has to do with the evolution of the welfare state in the twenty-first century.

When you look at the countries that have done well in the pandemic and compare them with those that have fared poorly, one factor that stands out is a given country's "strategic geography"; that is, how secure or insecure the country's location is, to what extent it takes direct and immediate responsibility for the safety and security of its citizens, and how these elements correlate with its management of the pandemic.

Take places like Taiwan, South Korea, Australia, New Zealand, and Israel. While skeptics like to suggest that it just helps to be an island, that didn't exactly help the UK, which had one of the highest per capita caseloads and death rates in the world. In fact, what the countries that successfully fought COVID-19 seem to have in common is a highly insecure strategic geography. It may turn out that countries that were already dealing with pervasive security threats, that knew they alone were responsible for their own safety, were quicker and more forceful to act, and had populations that more willing to go along with stricter containment measures. Ironically, it was those governments that ignored the advice of the World Health Organization that seemed to have the most successful pandemic responses. In the case of Taiwan, this was out of necessity—China will not let Taiwan have a seat at the organization, which means Taiwan can't get information about the pandemic firsthand. In the case of Australia, the government made a deliberate decision to ignore WHO guidance, which downplayed the effectiveness of border closures, because of its well-founded suspicions about China's influence on the organization.

To crack the nut of Canada's failures, it's useful to look at what the country did well in managing the pandemic, which amounts to one big thing: spending money. By some measures, Canada's income support for both individuals and businesses was the most generous in the world; it was also deployed quite rapidly. We also entered into more vaccine-delivery contracts than any other country in the world, though with relatively late delivery schedules. In short, Canada's overall response to the global pandemic was to rely on repeated lockdowns and to spend enormous sums of money.

What all this highlights is the underappreciated fact that *states specialize*. There are capabilities or capacities that some states do quite well, others that they do poorly. Further, the development or atrophy of these different

capacities is itself a consequence of a state's strategic culture and needs. We like to talk about the modern "welfare
state," but welfare isn't one thing. It's a combination of
needs, capacities, and priorities that includes domestic
security, national defense, public health, environmental
stewardship, and a social safety net. Some states priori-
tize security, others the social safety net. Few countries,
if any, do all of these things well, but when it comes to the
COVID-19 pandemic, it's pretty clear that those countries
that had a pre-existing need for control and ownership
over their own security managed things much better than
those that did not.

What the pandemic has revealed about the Canadian
welfare state is that it's basically a giant insurance scheme.
The global geopolitical lottery has made us rich, and
we've used that wealth to insure ourselves against enormous losses. What we don't seem inclined to do is take
the steps that would protect Canadians from those losses
in the first place. A similar analysis applies to the entire
European Union.

This might also be why we don't have anything close
to what more security-focused or self-reliant states such
as Israel, Taiwan, or Australia possess: a culture of collective self-reliance or focused sense of urgency about the
coronavirus. It might also be a big part of why we're no
good at logistics and why we've allowed our state capacity
to wither on the vine. We don't have to be good at doing
things, because we've learned over the years that it's eas-
ier to just pay other countries to do them for us.

This analysis is in many ways a recapitulation of our
earlier discussion of the phenomenon that Bertrand Russell observed, with our society shifting from a politics

based on the need for survival to a politics based on competition for status. Here, that observation is transposed into the key of international relations. Being rich and secure has made many countries in the West soft; unwilling or unable to make hard decisions and to execute the difficult policies necessary to properly manage the pandemic. For this, their populations paid a very high price.

And if this wasn't bad enough, the pandemic response of many countries across the West was also confounded by forms of partisanship, populism, and magical thinking that bordered on religiosity.

* * *

OVER THE COURSE of the pandemic, many Canadians and Europeans comforted themselves with the knowledge that, however weak and ineffectual their government was, at least they weren't the United States. And it's true that, by almost every measure, the United States' handling of the COVID-19 pandemic under Donald Trump was a pure distillation of his reigning mindset. From the knee-jerk "China virus" xenophobia to the hostility towards science and expertise to the conspiracy-driven denialism, the US took advantage of the global pandemic to turn itself into a barrelhouse of cask-strength populism. Trump himself was only too happy to lead the pub crawl, whether through his ongoing promotion of hydroxychloroquine as a miracle treatment or his bizarre recommendation that people drink bleach to prevent infection, to name just a couple of his insanities.

But the United States wasn't the only country to let right-wing populism drive its pandemic response. In the

UK, Prime Minister Boris Johnson implemented an early strategy of herd immunity, abandoned testing and tracing, and delayed any sort of national lockdown—to devastating effect. It was only when Johnson himself nearly died after he contracted the virus in March 2020 that the government started to take it seriously. The American populist response was more like that of Brazil, where President Jair Bolsonaro persistently downplayed the virus, calling it a "little flu" and encouraging people to just go about their lives, even while his health minister was putting forward a social distancing plan. Bolsonaro constantly called the disease a hoax, mocked those who wore masks, and told citizens that the vaccine could turn them into bearded ladies or crocodiles.

Even in countries whose pandemic response wasn't driven by a populist leader, public health officials' attempts to mitigate the spread of the virus were often confounded by various forms of grassroots populism. In some cases, opposition to measures such as lockdowns or curfews was motivated by economic interest or desperation. It's hard to support a lockdown when your livelihood depends on people coming to your restaurant, fitness studio, or hair salon.

But often, the public's objections to protection measures such as mask wearing amounted to a straightforward rejection of public health expertise and authority that bore many of the hallmarks of the alt-right. As an American survey about mask-wearing habits revealed, the refusal to wear a mask was closely tied to similar views on things like climate change—it was about identifying with a specific political tribe and showing your deep commitment and solidarity to the cause. At the extremes, this

involved an outright rejection of the seriousness or even
reality of COVID-19, a stance that was not greatly affected
by, say, the perverse case of Herman Cain, the Republican
activist and co-chairman of Black Voices for Trump in
2020, who died after contracting the virus at a political
rally where he pointedly refused to wear a mask.

Another disturbing feature of the West's pandemic
response was the emergence of anti-vaccine sentiment,
particularly in Europe, but in pockets across the US and
Canada as well. In a policy brief prepared for the European
Centre for Disease Prevention and Control, a survey of
major European countries found that only 36 percent of
Europeans believe that vaccines are safe. Depending on the
country, between just 44 and 66 percent of respondents
said they'd be willing to receive a vaccine that was found to
be safe and effective and that was provided for free.[54] In
contrast, as many as 70 percent of Americans said they
were willing to get vaccinated against COVID-19, while Canada eventually came to lead the world in its proportion of
the population to have received at least one dose.

What is politely called "vaccine hesitancy" has been
rising across the West for decades, undermining what is
probably the single greatest public health initiative of the
twentieth century. In addition to the measles, mumps,
and rubella (MMR) vaccine that brought those diseases
under control, we've also largely eliminated smallpox,
diphtheria, tetanus, hepatitis, whooping cough, and
polio. Chicken pox is usually harmless, many of us had it
as kids, but there's a vaccine for that now too, along with
one for HPV.

And yet we've been steadily turning our backs on this
success. The United States declared measles eliminated

from its soil in 2000, but the map of communities that are losing their herd immunity grows every year. Japan, Italy, France, New Zealand, and Ukraine have all faced significant measles outbreaks in recent years. The World Health Organization lists vaccine hesitancy as one of the top ten global threats to public health, alongside apocalyptic horrors such as antibiotic-resistant microbes and Ebola.

Where does this hesitancy or resistance come from? Researchers have identified two main reasons why people reject vaccines. One is the relentless media focus on anecdotal cases where side effects or deaths have been linked to vaccines, even when there is no causal or statistical reason to think the vaccine was the culprit. Another is the remarkable growth in "big lie" conspiracy theories alleging that vaccines cause everything from autism to infertility; the most insane version of which is the theory that the COVID-19 vaccine is being used to implant trackable microchips in people under the direction of Bill Gates.[55]

It would be a mistake to assume that vaccine resistance has a specific partisan valence to it. The truth is, anti-vax sentiment is one of the few things you'll find among both right and left extremists. On the right, it feeds into a long-standing rejection of expertise and authority, while on the left it finds a breeding ground in a resurgence of the Age of Aquarius worship of nature and its attendant hostility to science and technology.

The upshot is that magical thinking continues to permeate the West, to the point where it sometimes feels like the Enlightenment never happened. We're as religious as we ever were, only our gods have changed.

Conclusion: On Decline

ONE OF THE great conceits of the Enlightenment was that it enabled us to do away with religion—organized religion most importantly, but all forms of superstition, myth, and magical thinking as well. In his essay "What is Enlightenment?," Immanuel Kant famously defined enlightenment as humanity's release from its self-imposed immaturity, which is "the inability to use one's own understanding without the guidance of another."[56]

With enlightenment we grew up and said goodbye to the church, to tradition, to myth and superstition. All of it. In place of these things we have embraced the adult virtues of reason, logic, science, and evidence, as we became increasingly self-directed in thought and action. When will we be truly free? Only when, in a phrase incorrectly attributed to Diderot, we have strangled the last king with the entrails of the last priest.

We are certainly less religious today than we have been for millennia, at least when it comes to organized or established religion, though the process of secularization has not been all that even. Some parts of Europe report exceedingly low levels of religious belief and practice, the lowest being Scandinavia and the Baltics, where between 15 and 20 percent of the population say that religion is important in their daily life. In the centrifuges of the Enlightenment—England and France—that figure is under a third, while in Germany it is 40 percent, Spain 49 percent, and Austria 55 percent.[57]

In Canada, less than a third of the population say that religion is very important in their lives, and only a fifth attend church regularly. Those figures have been dropping for years. Two thirds of Canadians say religion's influence on public life is less than it was twenty years ago.[58]

The one big exception to the secularization trend in the West has always been the United States, which has long been an outlier in its public and private attitudes towards religion. But even that country has seen a startling decline in religiosity over the past decade. In a Gallup poll released in early 2021, the number of Americans who said they belonged to a church dropped below half the population for the first time. In contrast, there has been a steady climb in the number of Americans who identify as atheist, agnostic, or "nothing in particular."[59]

By all accounts then, Enlightenment values seem to be trending well across the West, especially if you focus on metrics such as church attendance and the general decline in expressed adherence to official forms of religiosity. But one question that rarely gets asked is, Why do humans have religion in the first place?

One theory for the persistence of myth and mysticism in human affairs is that we are biologically hardwired for religious belief. Our brains are almost certainly genetically predisposed to see patterns and find agency in nature. Many of our built-in cognitive biases are just fallacious forms of inference: we see intention where there's only mechanism, cause and effect where there's only correlation. This easily leads to the rise of cargo cults and the belief in rain dances and other animistic practices. But it does not explain why primitive animism gives us gods and other supernatural beings.

Religious belief, rather, almost certainly arose as a mechanism for the development and enforcement of morality. In small groups, behaviour can be controlled by strict moral suasion and external surveillance. As groups get larger, however, moral rules become harder to enforce. And so we get the invention of "all-access agents"—dead ancestors or the spirits of big trees, perhaps—who are always watching you even when the village chiefs or elders aren't around. Belief in pervasive external surveillance is eventually internalized, and people learn to police themselves. In our own era, the technique has been adopted by Western parents who use figures like the Easter Bunny, the Tooth Fairy, Santa Claus (and his in-house snitch, Elf on the Shelf) to encourage children to internalize norms of conduct. The world's three big monotheistic religions, each with an omniscient God at their core, are just elaborate versions of this original functional impetus.[60]

This combination, of a hardwired bias towards animism yoked to a mechanism for internalized morality and social control, would have been highly adaptive to both our hunter-gatherer and farmer ancestors. Any attempt at understanding why these useful delusions persist in the present day must take into account the way

they helped our ancestors with social cohesion and stability. That is, they helped create the conditions necessary
for beneficial collective action.

But like many of the biases that are part of our System 1 cognitive inheritance, dispositions that are highly
adaptive in one environment can prove terribly maladaptive in another. Just as our built environment
(especially the digital architecture of the internet)
increasingly resembles a casino, it is becoming obvious
that many of our major social and cultural institutions,
from health care and politics to education and the food
industry, are hothouses of maladaptive delusions. The
reason we don't yet suffer from these delusions is that
we're living through a unique period in human history,
one where our wealth and comfort has continued to
serve as a buffer against serious consequences related to
our survival.

As our beliefs have become disconnected from the
need for survival, they have become functional only to
the extent that they allow us to engage in various forms
of status seeking and tribal signalling. Otherwise, we can
believe literally anything, with no material consequences
for our lives. But as privately rational and self-serving as
these "luxury" beliefs are, collectively they are leading
humanity to its doom—it is the tragedy of the belief commons played out on a global, epoch-long scale. Economist
and futurist Robin Hanson has called our era "the dreamtime": an extended period where history is driven by
delusion.[61]

It's time to take stock of the argument thus far. We
began with the idea of progress as a package deal: that
economic growth, technological innovation, and political

emancipation are all just aspects of the same process of social development, shepherded by the guiding hand of reason. This is the promise of enlightenment. At the individual level, enlightenment means that we have left our intellectual infancy behind and become free and autonomous, rational agents. At the societal level, enlightenment is about escaping from various forms of tribalism and solving the collective action problems that kept us mired in something close to the state of nature.

For much of the last two hundred years, it looked like this promise had been fulfilled. We'd climbed a ladder and pushed it away, and progress had become permanent. But it now looks like the whole process has stalled and is even starting to go backwards. It's looking like we never really became enlightened. Perhaps we never actually climbed the ladder of reason, but rather stumbled upon an enormous orchard of low-hanging fruit. Feasting off that fruit gave us, for a time, steady economic growth, the worldwide expansion of liberal and democratic politics, and the steady arrival of technological wonders. But now those benefits have been largely exhausted, leaving us with stagnation in economic growth and technological innovation. This, in turn, is helping fuel political retrenchment and reaction in the form of nostalgia-based populism, tribalistic identity politics, and status-driven culture wars.

The COVID-19 pandemic is a case study in these trends at work: The detachment of science from politics, innovation strangled by a lethargic and ineffectual bureaucratic state, a population increasingly under the sway of magical delusions and falling into political tribalism—all of it exacerbated by the catalyzing hot house of social media.

The result? A society increasingly unable to confront and rationally address the problems it faces.

* * *

ONE THING WE don't really appreciate is how anomalous our period is within the scope of human history. Homo Sapiens has been around for approximately 300,000 years, and for almost that entire time we foraged, and, later, farmed, at something close to a subsistence level in a fragmented world with either a stagnating or very low-growth economy. And as Robin Hanson argues, while our ancestors "suffered many misconceptions, those illusions rarely made them worse off." Their beliefs and behaviour were, for the most part, reasonably adaptive for their world and their environment.[62]

This only changed within the last two hundred years or so, or 0.0007 percent of humanity's total time on Earth. Our current era—with its sharp rise in economic growth and tremendous pace of invention, discovery, and change—would be completely foreign to our ancestors of even three hundred years ago. But it's not clear that we are in any way better adapted to our environment than were our subsistence-existence ancestors.

Every human society has illusions of some sort. As the psychologist Paul Bloom has observed, across every culture, the most common leisure activity isn't eating or drinking, socializing with friends or family, or playing sports or games. No, "Our main leisure activity is, by a long shot, participating in experiences that we know are not real."[63] Left to our own devices, humans "retreat to the imagination," into books or movies or video games or

television, storytelling, even just daydreaming and fanta-
sizing. This, Bloom observes, "is a strange way for an
animal to spend its days."

Bloom suggests that the pleasures of the imagination
are non-adaptive in the sense that they have simply
hijacked mental systems that evolved for emotional
responses to real world events. He argues that while the
emotions we feel when we're told a sad story, or when we
watch a horror movie or read an adventure novel, might
be muted, they're nevertheless real emotions, to the point
where at times it's hard for us to tell fiction from reality.

This much is certainly true. But it isn't obvious that
the faculties for artistic creativity being marshalled here
have no adaptive value. These imaginative experiences
are unusually pervasive, and it would be weird for such a
widespread phenomenon to be completely useless.
Indeed, we've already witnesses one obvious outcome of
our capacity for storytelling, and that's the development
of proto-religious narratives as a mechanism for social
control. They're also useful, from this political perspective, for creating community and fellow-feeling.

Hanson, on the other hand, argues that our age is
dominated by "consequential" delusions that are neither
functional myths nor harmless entertainments. Instead,
we take our delusions for the real thing, to the degree that
"our descendants will remember our era as the one where
the human capacity to sincerely believe crazy non-adaptive things, and act on those beliefs, was dialled to the
max."[64]

* * *

THE COUNTERPRODUCTIVE OUTCOMES of our delusions manifest in a number of ways, some of which we touched upon in our discussion of the tragedy of the belief commons. But probably the most significant way is how our culture increasingly caters to System 1's capacity to interrupt or override the workings of reason, effectively turning many of our most important institutions into the equivalent of a casino. It's bad enough when we find ourselves lost in the supermarket or flipping mindlessly through the algorithmic offerings on Netflix, but in the political realm it has become utterly toxic. One side effect of our cognitive heritage, and the ease with which we immerse ourselves in fictional narratives, is our extreme susceptibility to advertising, fake news, conspiracy theories, and other forms of propaganda, much of it triggering the tribal instincts that underpin identity politics. This, in turn, helps initiate a vicious cycle of group polarization, where the narcissism of minor differences that is the hallmark of healthy democratic politics becomes the pathology of mutual incomprehension.

Which goes a long way toward explaining why the world is in such a mess. Civilization advances when people are able to set aside their private, family, or tribal interests and behave in ways, or just accept policies that further the common good. Many of the global institutions that were built upon the wreckage of the Second World War were aimed at resolving the myriad collective action problems that arose in the context of globalized trade and country's jockeying for position and influence. Military alliances, trade deals, transnational regulatory bodies, and many other organizations and agreements were the

building blocks of the stability and prosperity that characterized the post-war era.

It's looking like humans have reached the limits of our
capacity for global collective action. In Afghanistan and
other places, both the UN and NATO have been revealed as
highly dysfunctional and ineffectual organizations. With
free trade discredited and geopolitical tensions rising, the
world is retreating into protectionism and new forms of
mercantilism. It's been almost thirty years since the 1992
Earth Summit in Rio led to the groundbreaking climate
convention, but despite subsequent deals struck at Kyoto
and Paris, the world is no closer to taking meaningful
action on reducing carbon emissions.

And then there's the COVID-19 pandemic of 2020, the
first truly global pandemic in over a century. We had
ample warning that it was only a matter a time before
such a pandemic struck. We even have a global institution, the World Health Organization, whose primary
function is to respond, in a global, coordinated manner,
to public health crises. The wealthy countries of the West
all have large and well-funded public health agencies
charged with that same coordinating function domestically. Yet in too many places to count, these agencies
failed, in many cases criminally so. Any forensic inquiry
into our pandemic response must necessarily involve a
hard look at the decay in international institutions that
led to the shutting down of our economy, the closing of
our borders, and the ravaging our long-term care facilities, all of it causing untold damage to our students'
future prospects and the mental health of our children.

Our inability to take collective action in the face of a
predictable and entirely manageable planet-wide health

crisis is almost certainly a sign of what's to come. For so long, our wealth has protected us. Over the past two hundred years or so, thanks to relentless economic growth and a tremendous pace of discovery in invention, we've become rich in ways that our ancestors would find miraculous. To them, our age would look like one big party.

But this wealth has also shielded us against the most serious effects of our crazy beliefs and irrational practices. A species can tolerate a great deal of maladaptive behaviour when what it needs to survive and even thrive is just lying around waiting to be exploited. But now the free ride, and the party, are over. The bill is coming due and dreamtime is coming to an end.

* * *

IS THIS STORY of our civilization's decline inevitable? Not necessarily. As the hero of the Terminator movie franchise, Sarah Connor, teaches her son, John: "The future has not been written. There is no fate but what we make for ourselves." John grows up to become the leader of the resistance against the machines who are out to destroy humanity, even as the humans engage in a series of increasingly baroque exercises in time travel in an attempt to stave off the nuclear holocaust sparked by the machines themselves.

Sarah Connor is right, there are no facts about the future, and any one of the declinist trends discussed here could reverse itself. For example, the Great Stagnation could end if we discover ways of exploiting the higher fruits on the tree of growth and innovation. In his original essay from 2011, Tyler Cowen argued that the Great Stagnation might reverse itself within a couple of decades, once we figure out how to achieve genuine productivity gains from the internet and biotechnology. In a handful of blog posts and columns written in late 2020, he speculated that with innovations like the COVID-19 vaccines, the successes of SpaceX rocket launches and landings, and the rising affordability of electric cars, we might be starting to see the beginnings of a new era of sustained high economic growth and technological innovation.[65]

We may eventually come to grips with the deleterious effects of the internet, too. It could be that the reason the last decade has seen so much social damage from digital culture is that the human mind in the face of social media is similar to a virgin soil epidemic in epidemiology, where a new pathogen runs like wildfire through a population that has no previous exposure or natural immunity. Perhaps we'll slowly build up immunity to social media, and it will gradually become less socially toxic and politically destabilizing.

Finally, what looks to be a new cold war between the West and China might turn out to be a good thing politically if it focuses our leaders' attention on issues that actually matter to survival, while galvanizing people around the liberal democratic ideals that unite the left and right domestically and distinguish us from our authoritarian adversaries.

Any or all of these things might come to pass, and our future will once again be bright, shiny, and open to whatever opportunities and excitements the full speed of freedom might present. It's possible that science will find a solution to climate change, to the threat of runaway resistance to antibiotics, and to the enormous loss of biodiversity that we currently face. Decisions have consequences, though, and eventually a certain path dependency kicks in.

In William Gibson's *Peripheral*, the jackpot is a slow-moving disaster in which a lot of distinct environmental and economic shocks orbit around the central organizing force of runaway climate change. There is drought and crop failure, the collapse of honeybee populations, the extermination of large predators, and the failure of antibiotics. The jackpot crept up on humanity until it finally woke up to the crisis, at which point it was too late to do much about it.

If all this sounds familiar, it's because Gibson is as much narrating our present as he is predicting the future. Most of the shocks which make up the jackpot are already underway. But there's one aspect of the jackpot that hovers in the background of the story, like a sadness that's never really explained, which is the fact that four fifths of humanity was killed off in the span of forty years. For survivors, life eventually gets better as new technologies are developed for sucking carbon out of the atmosphere, along with huge advances in 3D printing of electronics, drugs, and even food. For the surviving one fifth of humanity, post-jackpot life is full of riches and opportunity along with an overwhelming sense of having dodged a bullet—the bullet was the eighty percent who died.

This story, of enormous scientific progress accompanied by broader civilizational collapse and widespread death and suffering could easily be read as a satire of our response to the global COVID-19 pandemic, as well as a prediction of how things will play out. Decline is coming, but it won't be evenly distributed.

And then there's humanity itself. While it might be hard to imagine a scenario, short of nuclear apocalypse, where 80 percent of the population dies out in just a few decades, if there's one aspect of our future that's close to being locked in it's the steady decline in the number of humans on Earth. Whether this is a consequence of women's emancipation, the struggles of affluenza, or connected to the incredible 60 percent decline in the sperm counts of men in Western countries over the past fifty years, there's a good chance that the world's population will stop growing by the end of the century and tilt into terminal decline.[66]

This trend turns the Malthusian nightmare of unchecked population growth on its head. China, currently the most populous country in the world, will peak at 1.4 billion people but see that number cut in half by 2100. Japan's population will fall from its current 128 million to around 53 million by century's end. These are just two of the twenty-three countries, including Spain, Portugal, and South Korea, whose populations are expected to halve. The global population as a whole is expected to peak at under 10 billion and then fall to 8.8 billion by 2100.[67]

In some ways this is good news, since fewer people will put less pressure on food systems and the environment. But as populations age, the ratio of young or working-age people to the retired and elderly will fall dramatically, which raises serious questions about who'll pay the taxes, fund the healthcare, and do the work. Maybe we'll follow Japan's lead of and have armies of robots run the economy, and even serve as companions or lovers. But replacing young people with robots will only underscore the deep existential nature of the fertility crisis. More than anything, having kids amounts to a bet on the future, and a civilization that stops reproducing itself isn't placing its chips on hope and progress.

Ask yourself, what are the chances all of this is just a passing fad? We keep expecting things like the economy, the environment, and our birthrates, to fix themselves, to go back to "normal." But it's increasingly clear that what we thought was normal was actually anomalous. The only remaining question is what happens next.

How will things look for our children a hundred years or so from now? The most likely scenario is that the future will follow the trajectory of the relatively recent past. Ongoing economic stagnation will continue to drive the zero-sum thinking that will amplify our polarized and identity-driven politics, which will in turn fuel a further decline in trust in liberal democracy. In social and cultural spheres, we'll find it increasingly hard to carve out a space for the exercise of System 2-style reasoning as the casino-fication of our physical and informational architecture continues apace. This will make it ever more difficult to resolve the myriad collective action problems that bedevil our domestic and international institutions. A steadily declining population means it will be hard to find the money, the energy, and the risk-taking we need to fix these problems. Each succeeding year will feel like the worst year ever.

This is not the end of the world. Decline is not extinction. Nor is it the end of hope or happiness. Our ancestors were generally happy, and our descendants will be too. There will be art and drama, music and comedy, love and lust. There will even be innovation and discovery—science and medicine won't come to a halt. But there will be a general sense of decay and strangulation and an increasing number of collective action problems going unresolved. Life will simply get more and more difficult every year as Earth's remaining humans retreat ever further into their various tribes. At some point we'll look back and realize that it's been a long time since things were any good, and we'll wonder what happened to the future.

This is what decline looks like.

Notes

1 nytimes.com/2016/12/28/opinion/2016-worst-year-ever.html

2 "Doomscrolling is slowly eroding your mental health," *Wired*, 06/25/2020 (wired.com/story/stop-doomscrolling/)

3 "We're probably living in a simulation, Elon Musk says" 09/07/18: space.com/41749-elon-musk-living-in-simulation-rogan-podcast.html

4 larrysummers.com/2016/02/17/the-age-of-secular-stagnation/

5 weforum.org/agenda/2016/12/charts-that-show-young-people-losing-faith-in-democracy/

6 theguardian.com/society/2017/oct/08/world-faces-antibiotic-apocalypse-says-chief-medical-officer

7 sciencemag.org/news/2017/05/where-have-all-insects-gone

8 slate.com/technology/2013/07/decline-of-wildlife-in-america-where-have-all-the-animals-gone.html

9 nationalgeographic.com/magazine/2018/06/plastic-planet-waste-pollution-trash-crisis/

10 bbc.com/news/health-53409521

11 mic.com/p/11-brutally-honest-reasons-milleni-als-dont-want-kids-19629045#:~:text=1.,people%20didn't%20want%20kids.

12 Joseph Heath's *The Efficient Society* (Penguin, 2001) remains one of the best introductions to real-world examples of the prisoner's dilemma.

13 Mill, J. S. 1977. "Civilization." In *Collected Works of John Stuart Mill, vol. 18, Essays on Politics and Society*, edited by J. M. Robson, 119–147. Toronto: University of Toronto Press.

14 the-tls.co.uk/articles/bertrand-russell-science-philosophy/

15 Russell, *Unpopular Essays*, Simon and Schuster 1957.

16 The others include *The Enlightenment: And Why it Still Matters* by Anthony Pagden (2013), *The Enlightenment: History of an Idea* by Vincenzo Ferrone (2015), and Joseph Heath, *Enlightenment 2.0* (2014)

17 washingtonpost.com/wp-dyn/content/article/2008/08/22/AR2008082202395.html

18 nasa.gov/press-release/nasa-astronauts-launch-from-america-in-historic-test-flight-of-spacex-crew-dragon

19 John F. Kennedy Moon Speech, Rice Stadium: er.jsc.nasa.gov/seh/ricetalk.htm

20 This is drawn from Charles Fischman's excellent account of the Apollo

mission, *One Giant Leap* (2019)

21 larrysummers.com/2016/02/17/the-age-of-secular-stagnation/

22 mercatus.org/publications/regulation/great-stagnation

23 GS reference page 1

24 In fact, in a number of blog posts in early 2021, he suggested the Great Stagnation might be close to being over.

25 Hall, page 99.

26 macleans.ca/politics/ottawa/can-justin-trudeau-get-big-things-built/

27 pedestrianobservations.files.wordpress.com/2019/11/costspresentation2.pdf

28 thenostalgiamachine.com/

29 afr.com/life-and-luxury/we-are-in-an-age-of-nostalgia-blame-it-on-technology-20150311-1418vr

30 For a comprehensive account of the deep structure of countercultural politics and its connection to consumerism, see The Rebel Sell: Why the culture can't be jammed by Joseph Heath and Andrew Potter (HarperCollins 2004).

31 voicesofdemocracy.umd.edu/buchanan-culture-war-speech-speech-text/

32 Bannon actually got the slogan from Andrew Breitbart, whose news website Bannon took over after his death: theatlantic.com/politics/archive/2017/11/how-breitbart-destroyed-andrew-breitbarts-legacy/545807/

33 One person who saw this from the very start was Angela Nagle, whose 2017 book *Kill All Normies* is an excellent exploration of the countercultural impulses of the online-driven alt-right.

34 Alheli Picazo has written a useful account of this, "How the alt-right weaponized free speech," *Maclean's*, May 1 2017: macleans.ca/opinion/how-the-alt-right-weaponized-free-speech/

35 A classic xkcd cartoon offers a pithy example of this attitude: xkcd.com/1357/

36 Rob Henderson, "Thorstein Veblen's Theory of the Leisure Class—a Status Update," *Quillette* quillette.com/2019/11/16/thorstein-veblens-theory-of-the-leisure-class-a-status-update/

37 Hall, page 178

38 This is a very popular view; one example of the general argument can be found here: steadystate.org/enough-is-enough-excerpt/

39 Give some examples. Heath and Potter, Robert Frank, Hirsch

40 scholar.harvard.edu/files/bfriedman/files/the_moral_consequences_of_economic_growth_0.pdf

41 It seems to have its origin in a short bit of satire from The Toast: the-toast.net/2015/01/20/next-black-mirror/

42 Becca Rothfeld, July 13, 2020, 10:26 p.m., twitter.com/@heideggrrrl

43 Heath and Potter, "Nostalgia for the Golden Age of Consumerism": cbc.ca/news/opinion/nostalgia-for-consumerism-1.3909789

44 thebulletin.org/doomsday-clock/current-time/

45 law.upenn.edu/live/files/296-kahan-tragedy-of-the-riskperception1pdf

46 The best systematic exploration of these ideas is Joseph Heath's 2015 book *Enlightenment 2.0*.

47 newyorker.com/magazine/2021/01/04/the-plague-year

48 See newyorker.com/news/news-desk/seouls-radical-experiment-in-digital-contact-tracing

49 "COVID-19 and the Swedish enigma": thelancet.com/article/S0140-6736(20)32750-1/fulltext

50 globalnews.ca/news/7697781/covid-alert-app-data-effectivness/

51 cbc.ca/news/politics/covid19-pandemic-early-warning-1.5537925
52 The auditor-general's report from March 2021 is exceedingly damning on
   this: auditor.on.ca/en/content/specialreports/specialreports/COVID-19_
   reflections_en20.pdf
53 "State Capacity in Responding to COVID-19": tandfonline.com/doi/full/10.
   1080/01900692.2020.1850778
54 forbes.com/sites/joshuacohen/2021/03/08/
   covid-19-vaccine-hesitancy-is-worse-in-eu-than-us/?sh=549165e2611f
55 webmd.com/vaccines/covid-19-vaccine/news/20210129/
   anti-vaxxers-mounting-internet-campaigns-against-covid-19-shots
56 columbia.edu/acis/ets/CCREAD/etscc/kant.html
57 en.wikipedia.org/wiki/Religion_in_Europe
58 pewresearch.org/fact-tank/2019/07/01/5-facts-about-religion-in-canada/
59 "US Church membership falls below majority for the first time": news.
   gallup.com/poll/341963/church-membership-falls-below-majori-
   ty-first-time.aspx
60 bbc.com/future/article/20190529-do-humans-have-a-religion-instinct
61 "This Is the Dream Time": overcomingbias.com/2009/09/this-is-the-
   dream-time.html
62 "Adaptive" here is meant in the evolutionary biology sense: A trait or
   behaviour is adaptive if it promotes an organism's fitness in its current
   environment, where fitness refers to the ability of the organism to survive
   and reproduce.
63 chronicle.com/article/the-pleasures-of-imagination/?bc_nonce=094dzfk
   dob8c1vjpbh2hmp4&cid=reg_wall_signup
64 overcomingbias.com/2009/09/this-is-the-dream-time.html
65 marginalrevolution.com/marginalrevolution/2020/11/is-the-great-stagna-
   tion-over.html
66 usatoday.com/story/news/2021/02/27/falling-sperm-counts-threaten-
   humanity-chemicals-blame-book-says/6842950002/
   See also https://www.pewresearch.org/fact-tank/2019/06/17/
   worlds-population-is-projected-to-nearly-stop-growing-by-the-end-of-the-
   century/
67 bbc.com/news/health-53409521